shop
local

A Practical Pain-Free Guide
to Shopping With Purpose

Heidi Butzine

SHOP LOCAL

A Practical Pain-Free Guide to Shopping With Purpose

HEIDI BUTZINE

Simplex Publishing
Redondo Beach, California

Simplex Publishing
409 N Pacific Coast Highway, Suite 260
Redondo Beach, CA 90277
permissions@simplexpublishing.com

Disclaimer: This publication contains the opinions and ideas of its author. While the publisher and author have used their best efforts in preparing this book, they make no representations or warranties with respect to the accuracy or completeness of the contents of this book and specifically disclaim any implied warranties of fitness for a particular purpose. The advice and strategies contained herein is for informational purposes only and may not be suitable for your situation. Please consult with a professional where appropriate. Neither the publisher nor author shall be liable for any loss of profit or for any consequences arising from the information contained herein, or from use thereof.

Ordering Information

Quantity sales. Special discounts are available on quantity purchases and for orders by U.S. trade bookstores and wholesalers. For information contact the sales department at the Simplex Publishing address above.

Individual sales. Simplex Publishing publications are available through most bookstores. They can also be ordered directly from Simplex Publishing: sales@ simplexpublishing.com.

ISBN   978-0-9826922-3-3

Printed in the United States of America

Cover art and illustrations by Angela Rubien

This book is dedicated to the remarkable small business owners and fellow entrepreneurs in my hometown of Redondo Beach and in the surrounding cities of Southern California.

CONTENTS

ACKNOWLEDGMENTS

I was honored and fortunate to have the support of many wonderful people to whom I express my sincere thanks:

To my amazing partner Erik Bowman for your enduring patience, encouragement and support on this project and in all of our ventures together. You mean the world to me.

To my cheerleading family for reminding me to follow my dreams.

To my witty, smart and beautiful friend Elaine Adolfo for making me turn this into an eBook so can actually read it.

To *ma chère amie* et *ma prof de français* Valerie Swanson-Parmentier for rediscovering the local culture of Southern California with me.

Special thanks to my special agents and local entrepreneurs for your enthusiasm and support to help make this book possible.

Jan McCarthy, my friend and *Entrepreneurial Guru* whose wonderful enthusiasm and generosity motivates me to keep growing.

Caren Magill-Myers who gave me the courage to turn my passion into a profession three years ago. Your writing at *Inspired Coast.com* reminds me that change is about balance.

Adele Sypesteyn, my business incubator buddy, interior designer and artist at *The All White Room* who's given me a greater appreciation for our local artists.

Susan Szudar, owner of *Sol Inspired* whose positivity is brighter than the sun.

Jeanie Rule, founder of *Solo Mama* whose warm hugs and words of encouragement at our agency meetings mean so much.

Anat Erez Fellner, graphic designer at *AEF Design.com* whose coolness and creativity are inspiring.

And finally, to all my fans and supporters who donated to this book project at *Authr.com*.

PREFACE

Confessions From a Reformed Big-Box Shopper

I must admit that I haven't always been a local shopper. I've spent my fair share of time and money shopping at retail chains, big-box stores and online at Internet retailers. I remember the first mega discount warehouse stores that opened up in my town. It seemed like my family spent almost every weekend at Costco or Sam's Club stocking up on necessities and buying plenty of impulse items, usually something indulgent like supersized containers of oatmeal cookies or a *ginormous* apple pie. To this day, I can still tell when something comes from one of these stores because it carries a certain big-box store aroma that seems to permeate everything from paper plates to a bag of oranges.

Although I've come to loathe the impersonal and sterile environment of the big-box stores and the super-sized offerings that feed our psyche to over consume, I confess that I still shop at some of these stores occasionally when it makes sense for me to do so.

In fact, this book will be carried by independent merchants and booksellers, but it will also be sold through Amazon and other online retailers because I want to reach as many readers as possible.

I share these confessions because I've learned that the secret to shopping local is all about finding balance in choosing where to shop and what to buy. And I've learned that it's never too late to start making a difference by supporting more of my local indie businesses.

I'm not an anti big-box activist or a shopaholic. I'm actually a reformed shopper and a fairly conservative spender. Shopping local has become more of a priority for me personally over the past five years, but I've always carried a passion for supporting local businesses even in my professional life.

As a small-business owner, I regularly meet with other local independent business owners and entrepreneurs. I've been inspired by stories about how people in communities have banded together during critical times to help each other keep their businesses alive. I've learned about the challenges that threaten local businesses whether it's economic factors, attracting more customers or responding to a demand to give the public what they want.

My travels abroad have also given me a greater appreciation for the need to support local indie businesses to keep our neighborhoods more vibrant, attractive and financially sustainable.

Through writing this book, I realize that a stable local economy needs to have the proper balance of big-box and national chain stores and small independents but in order to win, we need to do more to support local indie businesses.

Making an effort to seek out and frequent locally owned and operated businesses, has not only enriched my own shopping experiences by getting to connect with more people in my town, but I've also helped contribute to cultivating a thriving economic environment in my community.

Without getting too spiritual about shopping local, I believe that your actions influence others. Spending your money locally is not only going to impact your own life but also the lives of your children, spouse, family, friends, neighbors, clients, co-workers and certainly the business owners, entrepreneurs and even people in your community you don't even know.

Being a Southern California native who lives and works in my hometown, I take great pride in my neighborhood. I love the variety of businesses that are available to the people who live in or come to visit my town, so I feel an incredible responsibility to support and preserve the beauty and livelihood of my community.

Yes, I still shop at retail chain stores from time to time, but I've found a way to balance my spending to support more local businesses as well. And you can do it too!

INTRODUCTION

There it was in the town paper. The words leapt right off the page and hung on to my heart: GOING OUT OF BUSINESS SALE. The one place where I knew I could always find the perfect gift for my mom was closing its doors for good. After twenty-one years, the couple who started this sweet little gift store in a sleepy California beach town, usually teeming with local tourists, would hold their last sale, letting go of every item in the store—even the shelves built by the owner's husband that held up the books, sculptures and art displays that had attracted shoppers for over two decades...

You've probably heard similar stories about local stores, restaurants or boutiques that could no longer afford to stay open and finally had to close their doors. All of us can think of at least one place, if not more than one store in our town, that has gone out of business. Every place that closes has a major impact on upholding the sustainability of our local economies and threatens the livelihood of our neighborhoods.

But luckily this story does have a happy ending which wouldn't have been possible were it not for the support of local shoppers.

On the first day of what was supposed to be a weeklong going out of business sale, the couple opened the store as usual. A few passers-by came in to ask if they were truly closing only to confirm it was inevitable. Word quickly spread around town about this local gem boarding up shop and the following day, people flocked to the store. Some came to see the store one last time and some came to shed a tear and offer condolences to the owners. But something else incredible happened. The shocked and saddened customers rallied to support the boutique they'd fallen in love with years ago. Defiant to let the store go, the locals did what they knew would help the most—they started shopping. They bought up everything in the store until those shelves were completely empty.

After just two days the sale ended. But the store didn't close its doors. Thanks to the support of its loyal shoppers and neighbors in the community, this small local business had a turnaround. Humbled by the local support, the owners thought this could at least get them through the next couple of months to keep the store open. Two years later, the store is doing well and their shelves are fully stocked for their beloved customers who will continue to have a great local place to buy gifts for their moms.

Not all local indie businesses have been able to survive a comeback like the beach town store. My favorite burger hang-out as a teenager has now been replaced by a humongous megastore. Sacrificed to a bulldozer, this was a safe place in the neighborhood where I could meet up with friends after school. Today, many small local businesses like the burger joint find that they just can't compete with the national chain and discount ubermarts or the economy has made it impossible to continue to do business in their towns.

As consumers in the new economy, we've become more thoughtful, prudent and responsible when it comes to choosing what we buy and how we spend our money. Many of us might be feeling a recession hangover and are still reluctant to spend our money or we need to spend more wisely. Maybe we're holding back because we're looking for value and want to know that our money is going to make a difference in some way.

So how can you make a difference? You can Shop Local.

Shopping local is about being more mindful of how you shop. It's about understanding how to shop so that the money you do spend stays within your community. Most importantly, shopping local is about seriously committing to supporting the independent businesses in your area.

Regardless of your own personal financial situation, shopping local is something you can do to make a difference at any time. It doesn't mean you have to spend more money and it doesn't require making a radical change in order to make a difference. All it takes is a simple shift and I'll show you how.

In this book are stories and suggestions based on my journey to become a Shop Local maven and what I've done to make my own Shop Local Shift which I'm excited to share with you. This book mixes plenty of takeaway tips with juicy bites of information about Shop Local movements inspired by leaders of self-reliance initiatives and local business communities. You'll learn about the differences between big-box stores and local indie businesses to help you become a better-informed local shopper.

Shop Local is about aligning your actions with your values so that shopping local becomes second nature to you. I'll help you explore your own priorities and inspire you to focus on putting local indie businesses first when you shop in order to keep your money closer to home and benefiting your local community. I'll show you how supporting your local businesses is not only easy to do, but is economically and personally rewarding.

I've included resources and processes for you to use to determine how to make your own Shop Local Shift which is where you shift a portion of your spending by choosing to buy from local indie businesses rather than shopping at big-box, chain stores or online retailers. This book will help you set your goals for your shift and help you understand what your motivating factors are when you shop. It balances daily purchase decisions with making a positive impact.

Here's a sneak peek at the three parts of the *Shop Local* book:

LEARN sets the foundation to help you become a better-informed local shopper. You'll learn about the impact that large retail chains and local indie businesses have on local economies and understand where dollars flow within your community. You'll test common assumptions to determine your own values which allow you to set your Shop Local goals.

LIVE explores the values you live out in your everyday life and how you connect with your community. You'll learn how to set goals with the intent to create wiser and more meaningful spending habits. By setting daily intentions, you'll create personal accountability, learn how to make a responsible shift of dollars locally and take action to support more local indie businesses.

LOVE inspires you to find other ways to support local indie businesses in your town beyond shopping. It's about practicing your Shop Local values daily and doing a little more to make a difference and inspire others to Shop Local too or becoming a Shop Local maven yourself.

Being a good local shopper requires only a little effort on your part to become more conscientious of where you shop. While we can never turn back from the fact that we're a global community and able to buy just about anything online, we can still find the right balance to become better citizens and supporters of our communities which makes our lives more rewarding and enriched by shopping at local indie businesses. In fact, we may need this now more than ever given that we've become technology-dependent beings and often buy things without any human interest or connection.

If I can inspire you to take just one step toward shopping local, then I've done my job. I wish you a fantastic journey as you make the shift to Shop Local.

Readers of this book can access bonus materials by scanning the QR Codes in the book. Use your SmartPhone or iPad to scan the QR code (or enter the short URL in your web browser). You'll need to provide your email address once to access bonus materials. (Your email address will not be shared.) If you do not have a QR Code scanner already installed on your mobile device, you can download the free app at http://authr.me/cRU.

http://authr.me/cRU

SHOP LOCAL MISSION

I pledge to:

- Reflect on my Shop Local values daily.
- Get to know more of the local indie businesses in my community.
- Assess my priorities and create new shopping habits that will support my local economy.
- Be persistently mindful of where I spend my money.
- Take action by creating goals that are in line with my values and mission to help support local indie businesses.
- Create a Shop Local Shift that works for my lifestyle and priorities.
- Be flexible with myself when I have to shop at big-box or chain stores and find ways to balance those purchases with my Shop Local goals.
- Influence others to Shop Local however I can.

Part 1

Learn to Shop Local!

Foundation for Change

One of the reasons why I decided to learn more about the Shop Local movement is because of the people I know. The small business owners and entrepreneurs I've met personally and through my work are not faceless entities, they're real people doing the best they can to make a living like us all.

I knew that it was important for me to help support more of these business owners but I wanted to know specifically how and why. So this section is written to provide some background and create a foundation based on social and economic studies as well as the discoveries of some of the most highly-respected leaders of the shop local movement.

CHAPTER ONE
Why the Shop Local Movement Exists

Never doubt that a small group of thoughtful,
committed citizens can change the world; indeed, it's the
only thing that ever has.

—MARGARET MEAD

In order to understand why shopping local matters or how you can make a difference, you must first look at the events that have influenced our spending habits and why the Shop Local movement exists. The economy, *Walmartization* and local independent businesses versus big-box stores all factor into the Shop Local equation.

The evolution of the Shop Local movement is partly a result of many studies done over the years that have evaluated the impact of *big-box* and retail chain stores on local economies, jobs and communities. These studies show the value of small independent businesses and how important they are to the economy. They also raise awareness that larger chains and multinational stores are not ideal for supporting the long-term wealth of a community and bigger is not better.

While American Express has made it cool for shoppers to support local businesses through its recent *Small Business Saturday* marketing campaign, the Shop Local movement is not a new concept. For years, farmers, banks and credit unions as well as environmental groups have been promoting greater local awareness to keep your money closer to your community. Today's Shop Local movement is the result of a gradual shift in consumer awareness about where they shop amplified by the voices of local merchants. It all comes down to one primary thing—where does the money go?

Let's start by taking a look at the types of stores that we shop at and the differences between local independent businesses and big-box stores.

LOCAL INDIE BUSINESSES

A local independent business (or what I like to call a *local indie business*) is a small business that is privately run. This can be a sole proprietorship, partnership or even a privately held corporation. Local indie businesses are not part of a national chain or franchise brand.

Here are the most widely accepted qualifications of a local indie business based on independent business alliances across the United States.

Is the business privately held and not publicly traded?

If the business is a sole proprietorship or partnership with local owners making all the business decisions, then it's definitely a local indie business. Businesses and small corporations that are privately held, perhaps by the community or its employees, are also counted as local independents. Most national chain stores or big-box stores are publicly traded companies or corporations that span multiple regions.

Do the majority of the owners live in your state?

Even larger businesses that have more than one owner can still be a local indie business, but only if more than 50 percent of its owners are within your state.

Does the business operate out of a physical store or retail location? For a business to be considered a local indie business, they must have their own storefront or physical address entirely dedicated for retail commerce.

Is the business name unique or its own brand? For a business to be considered a local indie business, they should not be named after a known regional or large brand that it doesn't own.

Does the business have fewer than ten privately owned locations? Businesses with more than one location can still be considered a local indie business if they're privately owned and headquartered in your state. This is not to be confused with a franchise where the business is part of a national chain store brand and its operations most likely extend outside of the state or region.

If you're able to answer *yes* to all of these questions about a particular business—it's located in your town and owned by individuals who live in your town or is a private corporation based in your area—then it's considered a local indie business.

A Word About Home-Based Businesses

Most of the Shop Local movements—and a large portion of this book—focus on supporting local independent brick-and-mortar businesses. This is because small businesses that have retail locations represent a higher value to the community in which they do business based on paying commercial property loans for their storefronts and interest and taxes for their business locations.

Comparatively, home-based or online businesses do not contribute as much in property taxes as a storefront or brick-and-mortar business does. However, I believe that our small home-based business owners and non-hobbyist entrepreneurs are also an incredibly important segment of the business population which also helps to support our local and national economies.

As a small business owner, I do not have a retail storefront but I pay my business taxes and support and refer business to many other small business owners by choosing to buy from them or shop at their stores. These businesses should also be considered when you're shopping local but know that the brick-and-mortar stores represent the bigger financial contributors to the community.

BIG-BOX STORES

Over the years, big-box stores have become predominant in our communities. Big-box and national chain stores are owned by major corporations which are often publicly held and have multiple locations. The majority of the revenue earned at their various store locations often leaves the local community, going back to headquarters to support business operations, manufacturing and distribution elsewhere.

Big-box stores are aptly named after their physically large, rectangular box-like buildings. They generally have over 50,000 square feet of floor space dedicated to selling lots of different products.

As for independent retailers, they're generally much smaller than big-box stores. Many of the smaller indie or main street stores are less than 1,000 square feet. A full-service neighborhood grocery store is generally about 10,000 square feet. Locally owned hardware stores typically range from 2,000 to 20,000 square feet. And an independent bookstore might be around 1,500 square feet.

Here in the United States, some of the biggest big-box names are

Walmart, Target, Office Depot, Best Buy, The Home Depot and more. Big-box stores or *hypermarkets* like these are not only in the United States In France, they have Galleries LaFayette, Printemps and Carrefour hypermarkets. Other examples include Tesco and Argos in the U.K. Almost all of today's big-box stores are multinational, located in countries throughout North America, Europe, Asia and the Middle East.

According to the Institute for Local Self-Reliance, big-box stores like Walmart or Target "Supercenters" are the biggest big-boxes. Combining their standard merchandise with a full supermarket and other specialty services, they typically range from 180,000 to 250,000 square feet and their parking lots are often several times the size of the store itself.

Many other big-box retail stores—such as regular Walmart outlets, Home Depot, Lowe's, Office Depot, Bed Bath & Beyond, etc.—are around 60,000 to 140,000 square feet. Freestanding chain drugstores operated by Walgreens, Rite Aid and CVS are generally 11,000 to 15,000 square feet.

SHOP LOCAL TIP

Get to Know the People at Local Indie Businesses

When you shop at a chain store, you're just one face in a million and you may never see the same employee twice. At a local indie business, you'll most likely encounter the same people each time you visit. Get to know them. Once they know your tastes, they can stock more of what you like or even have items ready for you when you come in.

A growing number of cities and towns are adopting limits to store sizes to ensure that new retail development is scaled appropriately for the community and does not overwhelm the local economy or exacerbate sprawl and traffic congestion. Most communities choose an upper limit of between 35,000 and 75,000 square feet.

WALMARTIZATION

Walmart is one of the most prominent big-box stores in towns and neighborhoods around the United States and in fourteen other countries. In fact, the term *Walmartization* has now been applied to many big-box stores which have globalized and homogenized the retail sector or to those that hope to emulate Walmart's success for their own big-box store.

Started by Sam Walton in 1962, Walmart's first discount store was opened in Rogers, Arkansas. Although it was a far cry from where the giant company is today, it took only seven years before the company incorporated and added more discount stores in other outlying areas. By the early 1980s, Forbes ranked Walmart number one among general retailers for the eighth year in a row and the legacy of Sam Walton became a closely studied business model in many MBA schools. Walmart's success and growth brought its discount warehouses to almost every residential community across America and ultimately worldwide.

People loved that they could find a wide variety of items they needed all in one place at one low price. Why go to an appliance store, a book store and a clothing store when you only needed to go to one store? It was great for Walmart and for the consumer. But over time, it became apparent that the surrounding small independent and specialty businesses in town could not compete with Walmart's inventory and heavily discounted prices.

Given its dominance as a discount retailer, Walmart has been the focal point of many studies on the economic impact of big-box stores on local communities. The Center for Urban Research and Learning at Loyola University Chicago conducted a study in 2009 of over three-hundred local businesses located in areas outside of Chicago where a Walmart had recently opened. The study found that by the second year after a Walmart opened, eighty-two of those businesses had closed. The study also discovered that the businesses that were located closer to the warehouse stores had an even higher closure rate. This was an alarming fact for small businesses and this identified the need for even stronger independent business alliances and more support from the community.

THE ECONOMY

The economy is another major factor that has also influenced the Shop Local movement. Following the subprime mortgage crisis and the market collapse in late 2008, banks hastily tightened their belts lest they face the possibility of going under. This meant that the banks put a freeze on lending and the businesses that suffered the most from the lack of available funds were small businesses.

It's estimated that 99 percent of all firms operating in the United States are small businesses based on the latest statistics of the Census Bureau. The U.S. Small Business Administration (SBA) defines a *small business* as one that is independently owned and operated, organized for profit and is dominant in its field—having 500 employees or less.

According to Federal Reserve Chairman Ben Bernanke, from 2008 to 2010 only 40 percent of small businesses that applied for loans were successful in getting the full amount of money they needed. On top of that, credit standards became stricter. Money was harder to come by and getting the capital that a small business needed to operate became increasingly more difficult. To survive, small businesses needed local customers fast.

Fed up with the frequency of small businesses closing their doors, local merchants decided to band together and go up against the chain stores by reminding people of the benefits that small independent businesses bring to communities and the economy. You've probably noticed buy local or Shop Local signs and decals in many store windows. These are overt pleas by our local small businesses to try to gain support and survive the economic storm.

At the same time, more and more Americans were losing their jobs and now staying put in their communities. With house values at an all-time low during this period, it was harder for the American worker to sell their home, if they were able to relocate somewhere else, let alone find a job. As a result, people also began to seek local employment and looked to more local merchants for their everyday needs. This helped to raise greater awareness to support local businesses and preserve the communities where more people were now staying.

All of these factors combined are what brings us to the Shop Local movement today. Trying to figure out how to fix the national economy may be impossible. But making a difference in the local economy is feasible. Rather than pitching a tent to express frustrations about the economy, more citizens in our communities are using that frustration to rally support for local indie businesses and create stronger community alliances.

COMMUNITY ALLIANCES

Over the last five years, somewhere around eighty communities across the continental United States banded together to create Independent Business Alliances (IBA). These are community support coalitions made up of local businesses and nonprofits as well as local residents. The mission of the IBAs is to promote small businesses through practices like joint marketing, joint purchasing of goods, political advocacy on behalf of small businesses and public education on the need to support community businesses.

The American Independent Business Alliance founded in 1997 has helped other communities create their own IBAs and Shop Local campaigns. For example, the San Francisco Locally Owned Merchants Alliance (www.sfloma.org) now has over 200 retailers and service providers in their organization. The alliance offers support for local indie businesses by promoting them in the San Francisco area. Communities everywhere are urging residents to buy local. Places like Mt. Rainier, Washington; Great Falls, Montana; Fayetteville, Arkansas; and Raleigh, North Carolina are just a few cities that have also brought about initiatives to help create an environment to help small businesses thrive.

SHOP LOCAL POPULARITY

The Shop Local movement has gotten a lot of recognition and not just from the local merchants who are fighting for business on main street. The national chain stores are doing it too. Chain store companies that once maintained that shopping local didn't help the regional economy but that allowing residents to pay cheaper prices does help the local economy, have made their own "Shop Local Shift" marketing that they too are local.

One of the steps that Walmart has taken at some of their stores is sourcing produce from local growers to sell in their grocery departments. (Incidentally, Walmart is now the biggest seller of groceries in our country.) Whole Foods Market—another big-box store—features local products along with their other non-local items. As more big-box and chain stores continue to promote themselves as "local" to gain appeal with their customers, we'll need to be even more prudent when we shop.

Whether *local* is a term simply bantered about in big-box advertising slogans or if a chain store is honestly paying local producers to supply their stores with actual products that are locally made or raised, consumers need to be smart enough know the difference.

On some level, this might be raising awareness but let's think about what it means to Shop Local. It's about where the money goes and how much of it stays within the community. Local indie businesses help keep the economy thriving and create a strong tax base because their revenue stays within their communities rather than being sent out of the state or country to corporate headquarters elsewhere.

As shopping local becomes even more popular, it will be up to us as smart community-focused consumers to identify the local indie businesses and buy from them in order to have the best economic and social effects in our neighborhoods.

Whether the economy is thriving or depressed, the need to support businesses that in turn will be most beneficial for our towns and communities remains constant. Knowing what is local and how local businesses contribute to the economy is the foundation for becoming a more mindful local shopper. We'll take a closer look at this in the next chapter.

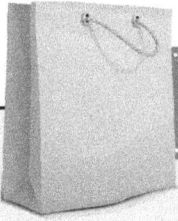

Community Comes First

Companies large and small can make an impact in the neighborhoods and towns where they're based. Two of my favorite examples of big companies giving back to their communities and putting people first is the Hershey Company and the Green Bay Packers.

Even though Hershey's is a brand that is known worldwide, it sponsors many local programs throughout the central Pennsylvania area and provides jobs for many of its local residents.

As noted in *The Small-Mart Revolution*, when the Hershey Trust was facing the possibility of selling to a major global corporation which would have meant big money for the executives involved, they chose not to sell and reaffirmed their commitment to the local community.

The Green Bay Packers is another great example of putting community first. They are the only community-owned franchise in American professional major league sports. As a safeguard to ensure that no individual can assume control of the club, no shareholder may own over 200 shares. And if the Packers were ever sold, the assets would go to the local Green Bay Packers Foundation to continue supporting activities benefiting education, civic affairs, health services, human services and youth-related programs. This community focus is one of the reasons why the Packers have never moved or left the city of Green Bay.

You can probably find other similar stories about the major companies that operate in your town. Buying products from businesses headquartered in your region, even if they are a global or nationally recognized brand, is another way to Shop Local and preserve industry in your town.

CHAPTER TWO
Where the Money Stays and Goes

Don't tell me where your priorities are. Show me where you spend your money and I'll tell you what they are.

— JAMES W. FRICK

We know that local indie businesses make an area unique simply because they aren't found in every town across America or maybe anywhere else in the world. Local indie businesses offer distinctive goods, services and experiences which leave their own indelible thumbprint in their communities. And so we want to protect and preserve the character of our communities.

But just about every business from retail chains to mom-and-pop local indie businesses use the term *local* in its mission statement or to describe its commitment to customers in the community. So how do you know what's local and where the money goes? Let's look at how *local* can be defined.

HOW LOCAL IS LOCAL?

Some say that *local* is defined as a certain number of miles from one's home or town which ranges anywhere from thirty or fifty miles to one-hundred miles, depending on who you ask. When looking at what constitutes a local indie business, keep in mind where the money goes. There are layers within the meaning of local based on where the business operates, its ownership and from where it sources the products it sells or manufactures.

Here are three things to consider when shopping local and making purchase decisions:

Locally Owned & Operated. You may need to do a little research to find out if a business is locally owned, but some of the most common examples are typically your neighborhood specialty shops, restaurants, personal or professional services.

Sells Locally Grown or Manufactured Products. Look for locally grown food products at your supermarkets and local farmers markets or find goods made by local manufacturers, artisans, creators or producers at your local retailers and specialty stores.

Uses Materials From Local Sources. Some businesses may manufacture their products locally or purchase the materials they use to create products for sale from local sources or businesses, thus keeping their entire operation local (and more green).

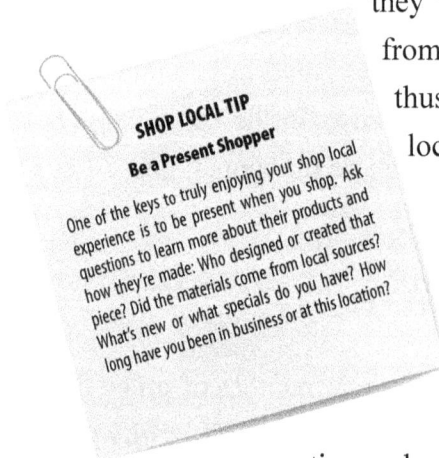

SHOP LOCAL TIP
Be a Present Shopper

One of the keys to truly enjoying your shop local experience is to be present when you shop. Ask questions to learn more about their products and how they're made: Who designed or created that piece? Did the materials come from local sources? What's new or what specials do you have? How long have you been in business or at this location?

A business may fall into all three of these categories or maybe just one based on its ownership and products. Keeping these three layers in mind can give you more options when you're looking at where to shop and what to buy based on what's important to you. For those times when you might not be able to buy from a local indie business, you can still try to be local about spending your money if you can buy items that are sourced from or are grown locally within your state or region.

Of course, society's reliance upon the global marketplace can make it challenging to find products that aren't made without some material that has been imported from another region or country, especially electronics. But shopping local is about balance and being mindful about trying to keep your dollars local when you spend your money.

Each layer will have its own importance to you based on why you're shopping and what you're buying. Let's say that you're trying to eat healthier and want fresh lettuce rather than the wilting romaine that's been trucked in from Mexico. In this case, you might place a higher value on something that's grown locally, so you buy your vegetables at the nearest farmers market.

Or maybe it's finally time to donate your worn out dining room table that you've been using as a desk in your office and get a high quality desk to inspire your creativity flow, so you head to the local flea market to buy an antiqued writing desk which has been painted by a local artist. For the desk purchase, you might place a higher value on finding a unique or used item that's created locally or the value is in the experience of meandering through a flea market and supporting a local seller.

If you can't tell if where you're shopping or what you're buying meets any of these criteria, just ask. Is the business headquartered in your community? Is what they sell or make local? Do they use local materials? If you can't tell by the label, then don't hesitate to ask an employee, the manager or the owner about their products, how they're made, or from where they come. They should be happy to share this information with you, especially if they see that you're interested in buying something from them.

THE MULTIPLIER EFFECT

One way to understand how a local indie business supports its local economy is through the multiplier effect. The multiplier effect is created when locally owned and operated businesses recirculate their revenue back into the local economy. The American Independent Business Alliance explains that the economic impact that a local indie business has on the economy can be measured in the following three ways.

Direct: Money spent by local businesses in order to operate, such as buying inventory and equipment, paying utilities and employee wages to local providers and employees who live in the community.

Indirect: Money spent by local businesses that recirculates within the community by buying from other local businesses.

Induced: Increased consumer spending as a result of local business owners and employees spending their money locally.

Based on the multiplier effect, when local indie businesses make money, they also spend money. And when that money is spent locally, it helps boost the local economy.

In the last decade, multiple economic studies have been done in communities across America looking at the amount of revenue that is reinvested into the community by local indie businesses compared to chain stores. A joint study done in 2004 by Civic Economics, the Andersonville Development Corporation and the Andersonville Chamber of Commerce had some of the most astounding findings.

The study concluded that the independent businesses in the

Andersonville district located in Chicago's north side reinvested as much as 25 percent more than national chain stores in the same area.

- For every $100 spent at a *local* business—$68 stayed in the local economy.
- For every $100 spent at a *chain* business—$43 stayed in the local economy.

The Andersonville study also pointed out that shopping at local indie businesses could increase a local currency flow by $25 more for every $100 spent. So if $100,000 is spent by the community at local businesses, then $25,000 more revenue is circulated within the region.

Another example of this is indicated in a study done post-Hurricane Katrina in New Orleans in 2009. The study analyzed financial data from fifteen local businesses and the local Super Target store. Results indicated that the local businesses returned an average of 32 percent of their revenue back into the local economy by purchasing goods and services from other local businesses. Super Target spent only 16 percent of their revenue locally. Since stores like Super Targets are part of a national chain, they purchase their saleable goods from their national centers and not from the local small businesses.

Statistically, these studies support the financial impact that local indie businesses have on the economy as a result of putting a greater portion of their revenue back into their communities. Taking the multiplier effect into account, not only are local indie business dollars staying local by paying their rent, employees and local taxes, but the studies also indicate that local businesses are more inclined to support charities and events in the neighborhoods where they're located or where the local indie business owners may live.

COMMON ASSUMPTIONS

So why are there so many of us out there who still have not made the shift to Shop Local? It might have something to do with the fact that we've made assumptions about it costing us more or we just haven't really thought about it much (which is why you've picked up this book). Maybe we've been led to believe that we won't have any impact at all. But when you choose to Shop Local, you're already making an impact. Whether it's a small shift to spend locally or an entire spending overhaul, doing more to support your small local businesses is making a difference.

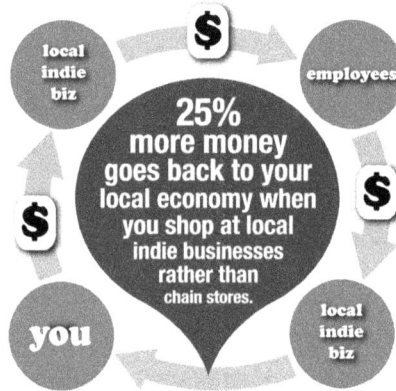

For you to make a Shop Local Shift that works for you, it may require looking at some of the assumptions you've made about retail chains and local indie businesses and reassessing your priorities and values. The following are three common questions I hear all the time about the bigger stores and how they measure up to local indie businesses on pricing, jobs and wages.

Are Local Goods More Expensive?

Whenever I talk to people about shopping local, the first question they ask is how much *more* money will they have to spend? But you don't have to spend more money to Shop Local. People tend to think that local indie businesses charge more for their goods and services than national chain stores. But I can tell you that after spending the last few years comparing local independent merchants in my community to large retail chain stores, this is not always true. Local merchants are often quite competitive on their prices. They have to be for their own survival.

In his book *The Small-Mart Revolution*, Michael Shuman cites a study which discovers that local independent drugstores offered better prices on prescription medicines than the CVS, Rite Aid and Walmart in a community. I put this to the test myself.

I did some research online to find my nearest independent pharmacy. I was surprised to find one that was less than half a mile from my home—I never would have known about this place if it weren't for my interest in supporting my local businesses. At my local pharmacy, I bought two items for $7.20. Comparing the same two items at my nearest chain store pharmacy, I found that they would have cost me over $14. That's almost twice as much.

One of the most surprising findings that supports the notion that chain stores are not as cheap as we think they are relates to how they go about beating their local competition. Some chain stores lowball their prices when they first move in to a community and then slowly raise them once the local competition is shut out. Consumers typically don't even realize it. In her article, *The Impact of Chain Stores on Community,* Stacy Mitchell points out that big chain stores like Home Depot and Best Buy don't want to compete with local stores—they want to beat local stores so that the chain store is the only option. And in areas where the chain store competition is light, their prices are also seen to rise.

What we find is that big-box stores sell the most common items that we frequently buy at the most discounted prices. This leads us to assume that we're getting a deal on all the items we buy from the same store. *Hmm...I bought the toilet paper on sale so that must mean that I'm getting a great deal on these sneakers too!* If you don't take the time to do a little comparison shopping, you may be spending more for certain items thinking that you're getting a great deal.

Do Big-Box and Chain Stores Create More Jobs?

One of the biggest benefits that retail chains claim to bring to the local economy is job creation. Because of their larger size and numerous locations, they claim that they will employ more local people. It sounds logical, except that over time, the presence of a chain store can actually cause a loss of jobs in the area through displacement.

When a large chain store opens in a neighborhood, many small local businesses are forced to close because they're not able to compete with the bargain prices of many big-box stores. Employees and small business owners then lose their jobs.

Evidence of job displacement like this was found in a study done by Emek Basker from the University of Missouri where nearly two-thousand counties in an area where a Walmart opened were tracked over a twenty-one year period to see how many jobs were actually created by the arrival of Walmart. During this period, Walmart claimed to have created four-hundred jobs for the people in those counties. However, the study found that when looking at the number of jobs lost due to displacement because of layoffs and closures of other local retail stores in the area, the number averaged closer to one-hundred jobs created during the first year of operation. The study also showed that, forty to sixty retail jobs continued to be lost over the next four years at other nearby retailers that couldn't compete with the discount giant.

So job creation is a numbers game. A chain store may create a job for someone in the local community, but at the same time it may cause someone else to lose their job. Or worse, cause a local neighborhood business to close.

Do Big-Box and Chain Stores Pay Better Wages?

You might assume that a major global corporation which makes billions of dollars also pays its employees better than a local indie business. But employing anywhere from 300,000 to over two-million employees requires the big-box stores to keep their payroll costs low to keep greater profit margins. Wages paid for retail jobs are already low and most employees are hired for retail jobs on a part-time basis which means that they might not even receive benefits. Plus for companies of this size, store managers are under pressure to make sales goals while still keeping down overtime and payroll numbers for their stores.

Stores like Walmart and Target have been criticized for paying such low wages. According to the UC Berkeley Center for Labor Research and Education about 65 percent of Walmart's U.S. workforce is paid less than $12 an hour. More than one-fifth earns less than $9 an hour according to their studies reported in 2007 and 2011. Overall, Walmart's hourly workers earn 12.4 percent less than retail workers as a whole. This *Walmartization* effect is not limited to Walmart employees alone.

Unfortunately big-box stores that keep their wages low also affect the wages of retail workers, grocery and general merchandise employees working at other retail businesses at the local and state levels.

For each new Walmart that opens in a state, the average hourly wage of retail workers in the surrounding state was lowered by two-tenths of a percent. Fifty new Walmart stores would mean a 10 percent average wage reduction. Wages drop because better paying jobs are replaced with lower paying ones. Since Walmart workers account for more than half of general merchandising employees, this reduces average wages noticeably. And competition in response to big-box stores forces local retail businesses to have to cut costs which often includes cutting wages.

Where large companies like Walmart can pay their workers less and still earn significant revenue due to their massive size and numerous locations, the local indie business is stuck not only trying to be competitive with the bigger stores on discount pricing to earn sales but they still have to pay their workers a living wage.

There are numerous studies to delve further into each of these assumptions and I encourage you to look into them to gain more knowledge. The takeaway point here is not to assume that shopping locally will always cost you more money or eat up all of your spare time. Test it out for yourself. Then weigh the benefits to your community and personally in order to start making a Shop Local Shift.

Big-box Detox

If you go into a big-box store planning to spend $100 and usually end up spending $700, it may be time to detox or cut back on your big-box shopping.

We often get seduced by the plenitude of items at big-box or discount superstores. What ends up happening is that along with buying TVs, tires and tuna fish, we also buy our fruit, produce and other perishables in bulk (all typically non-local items) and then end up throwing away unused portions later. We cannot fully consume these items when they're sold in such large quantities. And we have to spend more money buying storage bags, food containers or even a second freezer in order to store all the items we've bought.

Buying staple items in bulk at big-box and discount warehouse stores might make sense, especially if you have kids or a large family. But do this only if you know that you're actually saving time or money in the long run. Pay closer attention to how much you're spending and how much you actually consume.

It pays to do your homework before you shop. Be selective about your purchases at big-box stores. The stores are designed for impulse buys. Ever notice that there aren't any directories in the stores? This is done on purpose so you'll find more products to buy. That's why you find yourself bringing home a new barbecue along with your cereal, detergent and paper towels.

If you must shop at a big-box store or discount warehouse, know where you can find exactly what you need. Do the math and budget your shopping. Make a list and stick to it. Balance buying perishable items in more realistic quantities from a farmers market or local grocer. You'll feel better about actually consuming what you buy—and not wasting money.

CHAPTER THREE
Farmers Markets – The Original Shop Local Movement

Prosperous farmers mean more employment, more prosperity for the workers and the business men of...every industrial area in the whole country.

—FRANKLIN D. ROOSEVELT

The farmers market is one of the most traditional ways to Shop Local. Over 5,000 years ago in Egypt, farmers along the Nile brought their fresh produce to be sold to the locals at the market. Today, growers the world over gather each week to sell their produce directly to the public.

As weekly shopping at the farmers markets has become a ritual for some, many farmers throughout the United States use farmers markets as their preferred way to sell. There's no middleman or intermediaries to get their products from farm to table which means fewer hands have touched it. And since the food sold at farmers markets is locally grown and usually unprocessed, there are fewer concerns about handling and storage.

For some consumers, farmers markets represent ways to decrease reliance on food imported or shipped from long distances by providing adequate access to nutritious food. To others it's about protecting our food supply from threats to food safety and security as an alternative to a vulnerable food and grocery distribution system.

In the late 1970s, American farmers were allowed to sell direct to consumers thanks to the Direct Marketing Act. Over the past few decades, the popularity of farmers markets has increased the number of markets operating in the United States, clocking in at 7,175—and counting—according the latest figures from the U.S. Department of Agriculture. This figure has more than doubled in the past seven years alone.

In addition to creating new opportunities for farmers and consumers, farmers markets are dynamic social and economic forces for communities. They help revitalize downtowns or neighborhoods by increasing the entertainment and social activities available for local residents.

Some neighborhood farmers markets may be non-profit organizations that have specific goals such as increasing the availability of fresh healthy food for residents or creating opportunities for new local indie farmers. By attracting people to a farmers market in a neighborhood and encouraging economic activity, the community can be made more stable and vibrant.

FARMERS MARKETS ARE DEFINED BY WHERE YOU LIVE

The term *farmers market* makes us think of local farmers selling what they grow or raise to shoppers. But they can range from a small market held once a week with eight vendors in a church parking lot to a large weekend affair at an urban market with hundreds of vendors, entertainment and crowds of thousands.

Farmers markets are usually operated by a non-profit or government organization and held during the local growing season at a designated public place like a park or parking lot. Once or twice a week, a group of farmers sell produce and food they raise or create to individual customers.

The National Farmers Market Association recognizes only

farmers markets that offer produce grown within a thirty- to fifty-mile radius of the market. Sellers are someone directly involved in production (this is often relatives or employees), and are operated in accordance with trading standards, environmental health regulations, licensing, charters, and other relevant legislation.

How the term farmers market is applied to markets in your town may be vastly different from the farmers market downtown. This creates many local variations between each market's environment and your overall experience when you're shopping local.

In the southern United States, farmers markets are publicly owned and state-run where farmers can sell produce to consumers and at wholesale in large quantities. In the north, grocery stores and produce markets call themselves farmers markets although no farmers are actually there in the stores. In many public markets in large cities, there may be a variety of farm goods sold as well as local products, foods and crafts.

While the primary focus of any farmers market should be on the local farmer's income, there are also many direct and indirect economic benefits as well.

ECONOMIC BENEFITS

Over $1 billion of food and farm products are sold annually at farmers markets in the United States. This represents revenue for the farmers and the cities and towns in which they operate. By bringing people together to shop at the markets, other local indie businesses also benefit financially. Evidence of the multiplier effect also applies to farmers markets.

According to Project for Public Spaces, 60 percent of market shoppers also visited nearby stores on the same day they visited the market. Of those, 60 percent said that they visited those additional stores only on the days that they went the market.

Studies done over the past ten years show the direct and indirect economic benefits of markets from Iowa to London.

In Ontario Canada, findings supporting these figures show that shoppers going to or coming home from the market, visit at least one store during the same trip, and many visit two or more.

Reports from a study done by Iowa State University for the state's Farmers Market Association show that markets contributed as much as $20 million in sales to the economy and generated another $12 million in both direct and indirect economic activity.

For larger-scale markets like my favorite market in Seattle, Pike Place Market, and the Queens Market in London, other direct economic benefits include increased job opportunities and employment. In Seattle, Pike Place Market generates nearly $4 million in taxes going to the city, county and state with jobs increasing by 60 percent during peak season. In London's East End, the Queen's Market provides twice as many jobs than the local supermarkets per square foot and generates 55 percent more revenue for the local community brought about by the Market.

COMMUNITY BENEFITS

Farmers markets can revitalize a neighborhood by building community through social interaction and offering a place for locals to have fun. The markets can also help increase the ability of communities and regions to produce their own food supplies by putting consumers in direct contact with local farmers.

In many towns, farmers markets that started years ago at one location may now have several more neighborhood markets held every night of the week, such as the Green Markets in New York City.

Popular downtown farmers markets have also helped create vital long-term transformations both socially and economically for the community, some even becoming permanent public markets open year-round.

Other qualitative benefits of public markets include:

- Increased travel and tourism—also good for local economies.
- Increased consumption of local goods and services provided by various vendors.
- Improved quality of life and enhanced image of the neighborhood.

SHOP LOCAL TIP

What's a Certified Farmers Market?

A Certified Farmers Market showcases farmers that are certified producers, meaning that a government agency or official has certified that the market's vendors have grown what they sell.

While the qualitative benefits may be hard to quantify, they represent the importance of public markets in any regional economy. Many markets operate in neighborhoods where residents live on fixed incomes and in some major cities, farmers markets are critical sources of fresh food in neighborhoods where no grocery stores remain. Farmers markets also play a major role in making fresh nutritious food available at affordable prices to people with limited incomes.

MARKET SPONSORS & PURPOSE

To understand how farmers markets benefit your community, it's important to know who sponsors the market, why the market was created and what purpose they serve. Each farmers market has its own rules and philosophy based on the sponsor or organizer. Many markets are sponsored by the city, local governments, chamber of commerce, community development groups or by non-profit organizations, such as neighborhood associations or churches.

You might be thinking that the purpose of a farmers market is pretty straightforward—to create a place for farmers to sell their products and consumers can buy fresh local food. But the market is more than just a place for farmers to sell fresh food to people.

Education is a major focus for many markets. Making the public aware of the foods drawn from local farms, fields and waters, and raising awareness of the benefits of eating fresh locally grown or prepared and seasonal products direct from the farm, supports the importance of regional sustainable agriculture.

Connection is another objective as markets bring together urban dwellers and sustainable farmers to deal directly with each other rather than through third parties. They enhance quality of life by providing a community activity which fosters social gathering and interaction.

These are all reasons why we love shopping at our farmers markets, but one of the key challenges to running a farmers market is balancing all these goals at the same time.

Sponsors that focus on making the market an attraction for residents may be less focused on creating the market for local farmers and open it to wholesalers or peddlers. Markets focused on bringing better quality foods to low income residents may not attract enough participation if the market isn't profitable for farmers and vendors.

It's important for you to know this so that you understand how your local farmers market is supporting your community.

VENDOR TYPES AT THE MARKET

Each farmers market has its own rules for the types of vendors and products that are sold at their markets. This means that some products sold at a farmers market might not be made locally or may be sold by farmers but raised by another grower.

Here are some things that you'll want to keep in mind when you Shop Local at the farmers market.

Producer-only Markets. This tells you that the focus of the market is on providing an outlet for local farmers to sell only products they raise on their farms. The majority of farmers markets in the United States are producer only because it supports the whole idea of a farmers market. Allowing the sale of produce by those who did not raise it would be misleading for consumers and would create unfair competition for the local farmers at the market. Some producer-only markets may require their farmer vendors to let them inspect their farms to verify that produce sold at the market is farm-raised. It's also a way to confirm the types of products and quantity the farmer intends to sell at the market.

Carrying Vendors. Markets may allow farmers to sell limited amounts of produce raised by other local farmers. This gives vendors the opportunity to increase the products and range of items available for consumers. It also provides an outlet to sell for additional growers and producers of single crops, seasonal growers or those with short-run crops.

Crafts. Non-food items made by vendors may be subject to special procedures for selection and approval. Some markets may require that the crafts reflect materials from local sources or be made by a local artisan to be allowed for sale at the market.

Peddlers. These are vendors who buy products at wholesale for reselling at the market or to other vendors. Peddlers may sell items that are not necessarily local or produced by the vendor.

Prepared Food. These are take-away meals, snacks and ready-to-eat foods sold by vendors at the market. Some vendors may feature certain specialty foods made with local farm-raised products but prepared foods often contain non-local ingredients as well.

Processed Food. These are products such as honey, jam, vinegar, oils, cider and baked goods sold by vendors at the market. Most markets may require that these products be from a local source in order to be allowed for sale at the market.

It's important to understand these rules and how they apply to the products that can be sold at farmers markets so you know if you're buying local.

WHAT CAN THEY SELL?

Each farmers market will have its own personality and reflection of the regional specialties based on what's in season at any given time of year. This is why it's important to go to your farmers market throughout the seasons to see what they have to offer—from flowers for the garden in spring to amazing juicy produce in the summer and pumpkins in the fall.

Of course fruits, vegetables, and fresh flowers are important for many farmers because of their popular appeal with shoppers. The same is true with meat, poultry, eggs, cheese and dairy products—all high-value animal-based foods.

Some markets may not allow the sale of meat and dairy due to concerns related to how the animal was treated, how the products were processed or if it was properly inspected, stored and handled before sale.

This is definitely an important principle for many people and the individual markets will make their rules according to the philosophy of their sponsor and what the community wants. Some markets will allow these products to be sold because many consumers want to buy them when they come direct from the farmers who raised the animals.

Markets also know that the greater variety of products available increases the economic value of the markets for vendors because they're high-value items which generate better sales. As a result, most farmers markets allow for the sale of these products, as long as they're properly processed and handled safely. The rules typically require the vendors to know and comply with any applicable inspection and licensing requirements.

HOW DO YOU KNOW IF IT'S LOCAL?

One of the issues that often come up for markets is deciding how local their farmers must be in order to be eligible vendors at the market. Some markets may include several large neighboring counties or limit it to a specific trade area. Public markets run by municipalities or held on public property may be less likely to exclude vendors based on where they live.

If the market is a producer-only market, then there is no need for a rule on whether it was farm raised. But if the market allows the sale of wholesale items, then rules concerning terms such as *locally grown* or *farm raised* can be very important to help shoppers distinguish between types of vendors.

In places like Tacoma, Washington, vendors using words such as *organic*, *unsprayed* or *natural* are not required to be certified by any recognized agency but use of the phrase *certified organic* is restricted to only those certified by the Department of Agriculture. All vendors are required to advertise truthfully and to respond to a customer's questions in an honest manner.

WHO REGULATES THE MARKETS?

The rules of operation are determined by the sponsor who controls or owns the market. Each farmers market usually has a board of directors and may have committees that help set policy and the structure of the overall market. Every farmers market also has a manager who handles the daily operations and interfaces with the vendors and the public.

The market managers are responsible for ensuring that the rules are being followed by the farmers and vendors. This includes the market's own rules regarding conduct, liability and fees for which vendors are responsible, as well as rules that reflect applicable state and local requirements such as licenses, permits, health inspections and regulations related to food handling.

Managers play a critical role in the quality and integrity of the farmers market. They must watch out for vendors who game the system by buying cheaper produce that they didn't grow to sell at the market as *local* and cash in—called peddling. They must make sure that vendors aren't displaying signs with confusing or meaningless phrases, such as *naturally grown* or *no spray*. Managers also may visit farms to audit farmers and verify that their produce levels are in line with their reported farmers market sales to keep their farmers honest and maintain the trust of their local shoppers in the neighborhood.

GET TO KNOW YOUR LOCAL FARMERS MARKET

The best way to Shop Local is by getting to know the types of vendors at your local farmers market and what kinds of products the market offers. Be sure that you shop at those markets that have integrity and show a commitment to excellence. Here's what to look for:

Crops over prepped food and crafts. Pay attention to the number of vendors selling actual crops compared to how many craft and prepared food vendors are at the market. The more locally raised crops at the market indicates that the market is really focused on the farmer's income even though they may support other important community goals and allow other types of vendors to participate at the market.

Vendors are grouped by what they sell. Properly planned farmers markets and those that are certified will keep their crop vendors and farmers grouped together and separate from the non-agriculture vendors selling at the market. This keeps the markets organized and easier for shoppers. Note: Certified growers may be allowed to offer added-value items like honey, jam, salsa at their spaces, if they're made from ingredients of their own production.

Prepared food vendors are featuring the market's produce. Vendors selling prepared foods should not be selling any produce at their booth that is imported or is not from the local farmers at the market. This is direct competition and defeats the goals of the market. The best vendors will sell prepared foods made from ingredients sourced right there at the market.

The market manager. Get to know the person who manages your local farmers market. They're interested in hearing from visitors about the market and whether it's meeting their needs. Find out more about the types of vendors that are at the market and how they were selected. Make suggestions for local indie businesses that you'd like to see there as vendors. Understand what the market is doing to protect local farmers and how you can help.

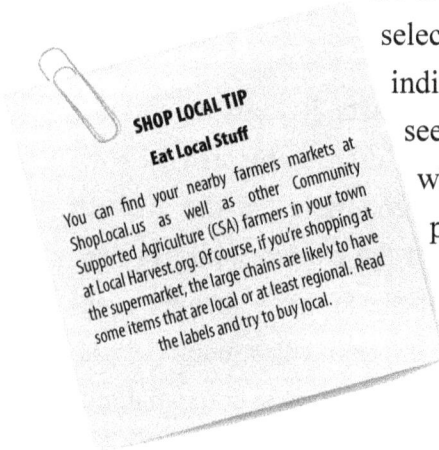

SHOP LOCAL TIP

Eat Local Stuff

You can find your nearby farmers markets at ShopLocal.us as well as other Community Supported Agriculture (CSA) farmers in your town at LocalHarvest.org. Of course, if you're shopping at the supermarket, the large chains are likely to have some items that are local or at least regional. Read the labels and try to buy local.

Be a Better Shopper at the Market

So how do you know if the people selling at the market are the farmers that actually grew the tomatoes you're about to buy? Can you believe their claims that produce is pesticide-free or organic? The best way to find out is to ask. So you know what you're buying and where your money will be going.

Here's how you can connect with your local indie farmers at the market and be a better shopper:

1. Talk with the farmers at the market.
2. Ask them how long they've been selling at the market and if they sell at other markets.
3. Get to know more about their farm and what they grow.

4. Ask questions about what's in season right now.

5. See if they carry any other products from neighboring farmers and what they know about them.

6. Ask the vendor when you don't understand a label or sign.

7. Walk down the rows and see what farmers are offering. If you see cherries when they're out of season or if it says they're from an area that seems odd to you—ask about it.

8. Get tips from other farmers on the best stands to visit and why.

If you're really passionate about getting involved and want to protect your local farmers markets, your state's Department of Food and Agriculture may have listening sessions. These are opportunities for the markets, managers, farmers, vendors and the public to voice their opinion on market-related matters.

COMMUNITY SUPPORTED AGRICULTURE PROGRAMS

Another way to Shop local is by buying directly from local indie farmers through Community Supported Agriculture (CSA) groups. CSAs have become quite popular in the last twenty years for consumers looking to buy fresh, local food.

The idea behind the CSA is that members purchase a share or a monthly subscription to receive a box of seasonal produce usually including vegetables, fruits and sometimes other farm products depending on the type of CSA.

Members can select the types of veggies and fruit that they like or choose to get whatever is in season. Some CSA farmers include the option to buy shares of eggs, homemade bread, meat, cheese, fruit, flowers or other farm products along with their veggies.

When selecting a CSA it's important to know how local are the participating farmers. Several farmers will usually offer their products together so their members get the best variety.

A CSA can be set up a number of ways.

CSA box delivery: The CSA delivers a box of items to the member's home and usually includes a mix of products that may or may not be based on member preferences, such as size of the household, how often they cook or eat vegetables, etc.

CSA drop-off points: Members pick up their boxes or select mix and match items at a selected location. Farmers may partner together to feature other items for purchase at the drop-off points.

Standalone CSAs: Offer specific farm products such as meat, flowers or eggs versus produce.

Third-party CSAs: Non-farming businesses sell boxes of local (and sometimes non local) food for their members.

Shopping local through CSAs benefits local indie farmers financially by having a market for their crops before the growing season begins. Upfront payment for subscriptions or shares helps balance out cash flow for the farm. In mix-and-match CSAs, where members can visit the farm to select produce for their own boxes, farmers have the opportunity to get to know the people who eat what they've grown.

For consumers, the benefits are not only eating healthier more flavorful and nutritious foods, but developing a relationship with the farmer and directly supporting a local indie business. The following are some things to consider before signing up for a CSA and how it affects your shopping.

Not all of your produce will come from the CSA. Since the produce is seasonal, you'll likely not get enough of the staple items that you use on a consistent basis in your household. Many CSAs may not provide fruit depending on where they're located and what they grow. You may need to go to the farmers market or local grocery store to pick up things like fruit, garlic, onions or potatoes based on the season.

Be prepared to eat with the seasons. We're used to going to the grocery store and finding whatever produce we want at pretty much any time of year. With a CSA, you can only expect to get what's in season. There are more plentiful times during the growing season where a CSA box may be filled with tons of produce and other times boxes may not be quite as abundant. Be prepared for times when the season is much lighter in production.

Know where the CSA farmers are located. This is especially important for the third-party companies that are selling CSA boxes. Depending on where you live, participating farmers may be quite a ways from your hometown. Your membership in the CSA is still benefiting local indie farmers in your region or state but ideally, find CSAs that might include more local or urban farms. Find out what percentage of the food they provide is grown on their farm. If the answer is less than 100 percent, ask where the rest of the food comes from and which items come from off the farm.

According to LocalHarvest.org, the government does not track CSAs, but their own comprehensive database now reports over 4,000 CSA farms in the United States There's much more information available online about CSAs. You can even learn about them from farmers at your local market who also participate in CSAs.

FARMERS ARE LOCAL INDIE BUSINESSES TOO

Farmers markets and local CSAs are important to the Shop Local movement because they give local farmers the chance to sell food they raise directly to customers and they allow consumers to buy fresh food from the farmers who raise it.

As local indie businesses, farmers use the markets as a way to test market and experiment with new products or unique crops to gauge consumer interest. Farmers markets help create new farms and food businesses by giving small farm-based businesses the chance to use the markets as their launching pad for expanding their operations. In my home state of California, more than 20 percent of the vendors at farmers markets have expanded to distribute their produce through direct sales to restaurants, as suppliers to secondary and tertiary markets, and to members of Community Supported Agriculture groups. This helps support local and state economies.

The markets provide ways to create community excitement and activity in downtowns and neighborhoods. Both farmers markets and CSAs give us all the opportunity to think about what goes into our food supply and how we can keep it local. And most importantly, they keep our money circulating very closely within our community and going directly to the local indie farmers. All of these are powerful reasons why you should support your local farmers and one of the best ways to Shop Local.

In this section, you've learned about some of the background behind the Shop Local movement and hopefully see that investing in our own communities is something we should all be doing in some way. A Shop Local Shift can help bring about greater economic recovery and sustain local economies for the long run. That's why it's imperative to support your friends and neighbors in your small business community by shopping local. Now that you've established the foundation for becoming a more mindful local shopper, it's time to take these concepts to heart and adopt this information into your life. Now let's learn how to LIVE to Shop Local.

Start With One Item

Making a change to shop local is best started by keeping things simple. Begin by choosing just one item to focus on buying locally. And then add more when you're ready.

Maybe this month, you have an upcoming birthday for a friend or family member, so you decide to buy a gift or present them with a gift certificate from a local shop instead of a chain store. Or the new bakery that has been wafting out smells of fresh-baked bread at you while you pass by during your morning run inspires you to pick up a baguette on the way home rather than buying bread at the supermarket.

These may seem to be simple ideas but making even the smallest choices to shop local will motivate you to keep finding other ways to spend your dollars locally.

Here are some other examples of items you can easily add to your Shop Local Shift: food and produce, gifts, personal care items, home repair items, clothing, books and home décor items.

Part 2

Live to Shop Local!

Taking Action Daily

When I started down the path to Shop Local, one of the things I needed to do is become more in tune with why I wanted to make a shift and how I could do it without driving myself crazy. See, I'm the type of person who can get pretty obsessive about things for which I'm passionate like shopping local. Just to give you some idea, when I started setting my own goals to buy from local indie businesses, my mind was swimming with questions like: How do I decide where to shop? Should I switch to a local bank? Where can I buy underwear locally? Should I feel bad about shopping at major retail chains? These questions helped me discover that I needed to find balance. They also helped me discover what motivates me and what dictates my priorities when I shop.

I decided I would do my best to support local indie businesses and think of them first whenever I shopped—my own Shop Local goal. But I would not beat myself up for those times when I might have to buy from a chain store.

You may not have the same crazy questions like mine, but in this next section, you'll do some homework to discover your own values, priorities and motivators to help you live out your Shop Local goals.

CHAPTER FOUR
Create Your Mission and Action Plan

One person can make a difference, and everyone should try.

—JOHN F. KENNEDY

So how can you make your own Shop Local Shift to support more indie businesses in your town? By setting some goals and creating a plan that works for you. Like any mission that you set out to achieve, you need to reflect on your own values (real or desired). First, start by thinking about what matters most to you regarding your lifestyle and budget, your family needs and personal needs, and your commitment to your community. These are your values and motivators. In this section, I'll share with you the process that has helped me make my own Shop Local Shift to may help you with yours.

I've created a Shop Local Shift Planner that you can also use for this process. Scan the QR code here using your SmartPhone or iPad to download the Planner tool (or enter the URL in your web browser). This Planner will help you track your goals and keep you focused on how you're doing with your Shop Local Shift.

http://authr.me/cRT

EXPLORE YOUR VALUES

We all have our own values that guide us in making everyday decisions and lead us to taking action. These are the principles that help us set goals, pursue our passion and get things accomplished. The following questions will help you start exploring your Shop Local values. Grab a piece of paper, open up the Shop Local Planner or start a new note on your iPad and jot down your thoughts for each of these questions:

1. What are the things that you love about your community?
2. Which of those things would you miss most if they were gone?
3. Why do you want to Shop Local?
4. What are your personal, economic, environmental or community goals?
5. Do you envision inspiring others through your actions or choices?
6. Would you like to leave a legacy for supporting your community?

By thinking about each of these questions, you can better understand what it really is that motivates you. This will allow you to focus on setting priorities to meet your Shop Local goals. Your answers to each of these questions serve as the foundation for shopping local and will guide your actions and purchase decisions that you make each day.

KNOW YOUR SHOPPING HABITS

If you want to make a Shop Local Shift happen, then you may have to change some of your habits and behaviors. We sometimes shop at the same old places and buy the same things week after week or each month out of habit. It becomes so tedious that we often end up spending our money on the same necessities without paying attention to how much we're spending or assume that we're always getting the same great deals.

Some of us may splurge here and there to buy something special and may not look at the big picture and what's in the budget. Taking a look at your own shopping habits and how you're spending your money is part of making a Shop Local Shift. This process has helped me reach my goals by making me more aware of how I spend my money, actually helping me spend smarter.

So get a clean sheet of paper on your notepad or use your Planner and consider the following questions:

1. What am I currently spending my money on now?
2. Where am I shopping or spending my money?
3. How can I cut down on some of my purchases from non-local businesses?
4. What purchases do I know I can buy locally, starting immediately?

Being very clear about your shopping habits makes it easier for you to make meaningful choices about how you spend your money. Your answers to these questions should start to show you what actionable steps you can take today to create your mission and support your pledge to Shop Local.

How you spend your time and money is a direct reflection of your values. Your purchase decisions may be reactive or impulse driven, other times they may be proactive. This review is meant to help you become more proactive and mindful when making purchase decisions.

ESTABLISH YOUR PRIORITIES

Once you know your values and habits you can set your priorities. Be honest and ask yourself if the activities that take up most of your time really are moving you toward your goals. If not, it's time to set some priorities that will support your mission and enable you to reach your goals.

We all have different priorities when it comes to deciding what we buy, where we shop, how much we want to spend and why we need to buy something. Most of our priorities can be boiled down to the value we place on *time, money* and *happiness*. Some people must always get the best deals or hunt for bargains. Some simply want to get their shopping done and over with quickly. Others want to enjoy the experience of shopping.

Your priorities dictate your actions and they will change based on what matters to you most at any given time when you shop. You might choose to drive a little farther to shop at a local store because you know that the exceptional service is worth the extra time or gas money you spend to get there (*happiness*). Or you may have to rush to the supermarket to buy diapers for the little one before you run out of them (*time*). Maybe you're not able to save for a get-away to Tuscany this year, so you opt for a staycation instead (*money*). All of these factors—*time, money* and *happiness*—are part of the Shop Local decisions that you make.

Below are three of the most common factors that often dictate some of our Shop Local priorities. These questions will help you think about what's most important to you when it comes to how you spend your time and money.

How far are you willing to drive? Sometimes we make decisions on where to shop because of the proximity to our home or work. If the chain store is right down the street, but a local independent merchant is ten blocks away, you may not be willing to go the extra distance to Shop Local. And that's perfectly fine. But sometimes, our narrow focus can cause us to miss the best local stores in our community. You may find the few extra miles and the time it takes to get there is worth it because your choice to buy from a local indie business makes you feel better and supports your Shop Local mission.

How much are you willing to pay? A budget isn't the only thing that dictates why we buy something and what we're willing to spend. Logical, emotional and hidden motivators can play into our decisions, such as time, comfort, fun, prestige, health or exclusivity which affects how much we decide we can spend on something we want to buy. It's good to be aware of these motivators when you're shopping local and how to use them to support your goals.

SHOP LOCAL TIP

Who's Local?

An easy way to make the Shop Local Shift is to look for some of the most common types of local indie businesses around town. Buy from local indie... hair salons, nail salons, florists, accountants, dry cleaners, pharmacies, auto repair shops, bakeries, coffee shops, diners & restaurants, hardware stores, photocopy services, bookstores, bicycle shops, children's boutiques, home furnishings, gift shops, clothing boutiques, antique stores, second-hand clothing stores and more.

What kind of service or experience is important to you? Some of us like to enter a store, find what we need and then leave without asking a single employee for help. (This is how I used to shop.) Others like to be helped when we're shopping so we don't have to waste time searching for what we need. Whatever shopping type you may be, I think you'll that find shopping local can improve how you spend your time and your overall shopping experience. I find that local stores are often more attentive—their store employees are easier for me to find and they generally know their products and services very well. I've also seen my local stores go the extra mile to order items or customize their products for me. Local independents count on each person who shops in their stores to keep their businesses alive, so I find that they try a little harder to keep me coming back.

SET YOUR GOALS

The key to success is to set some achievable and realistic goals. Sitting down and putting your goals to paper or screen is not easy. But you have to take this first step in order to get to where you want to be.

Go back to your notepad or Planner where you wrote down some of your Shop Local values. Think about the things that you spend your money on the most. Now list the top five things that you spend your money on during an average week. Next to each item, mark which of those things that you buy from local indie businesses versus chain stores. This will help you determine how satisfied you are with your current spending habits and assess whether it aligns with how you want to Shop Local.

Based on what you've learned earlier in this book about local indie businesses, you may realize that you're spending your money more locally than you first thought. Perhaps you find that you want to do more. Terrific! But if you're not carrying out your Shop Local mission in your day-to-day actions, that's okay. It's never too late to set goals for your Shop Local Shift. And you don't have to tackle all of them at once.

Remember, this book is about keeping it simple and starting to make a shift that matters most to you and your community. My mission is to help you find ways to reach your Shop Local goals and make the changes you want. If you seem to be doing alright, then maybe there's a bigger goal that set for yourself or you might want to get more involved by being a Shop Local champion in your community.

Now go back and list your top five wish-list purchases that you'd like to make in the near future. This could be anything you like—a massage, gear for weekend bike rides, new bedding or a book for the kids. Think about your values for shopping local. Now think about ways that you can incorporate a few of those wish-list items into your Shop Local list and set some goals.

You might be thinking, *I'll just read this book and skip the homework.* Maybe you decide that you'll shift $50 of your budget to spend at local businesses each month. That's a great start! But for how long do you think you can keep it up? What happens if you forget? Will you let yourself slide and remember to make it up next month? This is why you might want to consider setting some goals.

Making the extra effort to create a plan puts you on the path for success. Plus, you'll get the joy of being able to look back at what you've achieved with your Shop Local Shift and relish how great it feels to be supporting your local economy.

Taking this process to heart will help you get clear about your own values and goals and allows you to adopt this information into your life and LIVE to Shop Local.

Why Do We Buy?

Knowing the motivators behind why you buy is really helpful when you're setting Shop Local goals. Motivators are logical and emotional drivers that factor into all of your buying decisions. For example: *I want to shop local because I need something* is a logical motivator. *I shop local because I feel guilty for not supporting my local businesses* is an example of an emotional motivator. But there are also "hidden" motivators for buying which could be related to both.

- Time — for yourself, your family, your interests
- Comfort — convenience, ease, luxury, self-indulgence
- Money — to save, to spend, to give to others
- Popularity — to be liked by friends, family, and significant others
- Praise — for intelligence, knowledge, appearance, and other superior qualities
- Pride of accomplishment — doing things well, overcoming obstacles and competition
- Self-confidence — to feel worthy, at-ease, physically or mentally superior
- Security — at home, in old age, financial independence, provisions for age or adversity
- Leisure — for travel, hobbies, rest, play, self-development
- Fun — feeling like a kid again, doing something for no good reason, goofing off
- Prestige — feeling of importance, a member of a select group, having power
- Enjoyment — food, drink, entertainment, other physical contacts
- Health — strength, vigor, endurance, longer life
- Better appearance — beauty, style, physical build, cleanliness
- Exclusivity — being in on something special
- Envy — having something others desire

- Ego Gratification — to support or enhance self-image
- Business advancement — feeling successful, getting a better job, being one's own boss
- Social advancement — keeping up with neighbors, moving in desirable social circles

There is no way to know exactly what emotion will trigger your Shop Local decisions in any given situation. In most cases, there are several hidden motivators working at once. But with a little thought, you can probably identify a handful of hidden motivators at play. Once you've focused in on your main motivators and you know why you're buying, you can create Shop Local goals that are most meaningful to you.

CHAPTER FIVE
Your Shop Local Shift Tool Kit

Whenever you want to achieve something, keep your eyes open, concentrate and make sure you know exactly what it is you want. No one can hit their target with their eyes closed.

— PAULO COELHO

Making a spending shift to Shop Local doesn't require you to spend more money. A Shop Local Shift is taking a portion of the money that you're already spending and choosing to spend it purposefully at local indie businesses rather than at national chain or big-box stores, whenever you can. It's really not that hard to do. It takes only a few minutes over a cup of tea or glass of wine to figure out how much of a shift you want to make.

I've included a Shop Local Shift Calculator to help you with this. Scan the QR code here using your SmartPhone or iPad (or enter the URL in your web browser) to use the calculator.

http://authr.me/cRR

SHOP LOCAL SHIFT CALCULATOR

One of the smartest ways to go about making a Shop Local Shift is by committing to spending a certain percentage of your annual budget at local indie businesses.

To choose a spending shift that's right for you, start by looking at how much you spend each year. Then set an amount that you want to shift to spending at local indie businesses each month or you can just focus on a few areas of your budget to shift locally.

The Shop Local Shift Calculator will help you determine how much you're spending in each area of your budget. You'll estimate how much you're already spending locally. Then you'll decide how much you want to shift to shopping local. You can choose to shift 1 percent, 5 percent, 10 percent or just $50 a month. The calculator will help you set new budget goals based on your Shop Local Shift.

SHOP LOCAL TIP

Switch to Local Banks

Banking at an local indie bank or credit union is a great way to help support your community. Community banks typically lend to the most local neighborhood businesses and families in your community, so by keeping your money at a local financial institution rather than a national bank, you're also indirectly supporting growth of the local indie businesses in your community.

You may find that you can go above and beyond making a 10 percent or a $50 shift every month.

How much you shift is all up to you. Any shift to Shop Local is good. So get started by making these changes where you can and take action.

Regardless of whether you're a budgeting guru or if the idea of managing a budget just makes you cringe, it's a good idea to sit down and look at your spending every month. Using your Shop Local Calculator and Planner, look at how you're doing with your spending shift and your goals. Doing this can actually end up saving you a lot of stress and concern about money and your spending habits. By having a focus on how you're going to Shop Local, it makes the

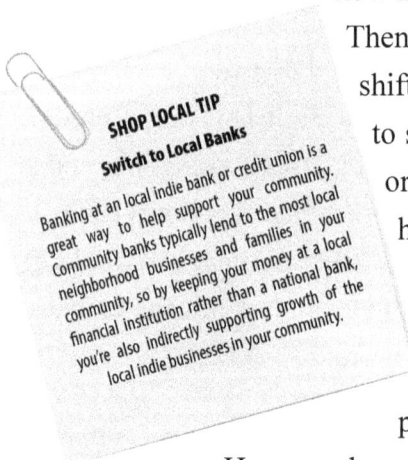

budget review process a little easier and much more rewarding since you can look at what you've accomplished each month!

FOCUS ON FIVE

When you shift your spending, you're more likely to be successful if you can make this shift gradually. So I recommend picking a few key areas of spending that will be the easiest or most motivating for you to try shift locally first. If you find that you still need to shop every now and then at retail chains or big-box stores, that's okay. Just start to make the shift. Then keep looking for other areas that you can incorporate along the way.

1. **Your Food Budget.** Food is probably one of the easiest expenses to shift to shopping local. This can be done by buying locally raised produce, meat or dairy products, by visiting a farmers market in your neighborhood. If you can't get to a farmers market, try to select produce at your grocery store that is at least grown in-state versus outside of the country or sign up for a Community Supported Agriculture (CSA) membership to receive seasonal produce each week direct from the farms. Another easy way to shift spending on more local food is by eating out at a local indie restaurant over a fast-food or large chain restaurant. If you don't know whether your local restaurant is a franchise or national chain, you can usually tell by visiting the company website and looking at the about us page to see their ownership structure. I've been surprised by how many restaurants that I thought were local are actually part of a larger group of chain restaurants owned by a corporation based in another state. So check them out first and go to the restaurants

you know are local and independently owned.

2. **Home Services.** You probably spend a fair amount of your budget on maintaining your home throughout the year or paying for unexpected repairs. Whether hiring a gardener, pool cleaner, plumber, electrician, housekeeping or repair services. Take a look at the businesses or contractors available to you in your town. Are they a local indie professional? Or are they part of a franchise or a national company? Can you make the shift to employ a local service provider instead? Some of the resources that have helped me find local home services are Yelp.com as well as Angieslist.com and ServiceMagic. com. These sites not only list the local service providers in your area, they also provide consumer reviews so you can read what people have to say about their services before you hire them.

3. **Professional Services.** This category includes professional services such as tax accountants, financial planners, attorneys and even medical professionals like doctors and dentists. Try to find professionals who are sole practitioners, are part of a local partnership or a local group cooperative. Professionals like these are in every town so they're relatively easy to find online. Ask for referrals from your friends and neighbors or find them through your local chamber of commerce.

4. **Personal Services.** Don't forget about your own personal needs. Even when you're on a tight budget, you still need to spend a little money on yourself every year. Whether you visit a hair salon, barber shop, nail salon,

day spa or go to the gym. Try to use local indie businesses for personal services. They're generally competitive with their pricing and are likely to offer rewards to loyal customers or referrals to their local business.

5. **Your Entertainment Budget.** Take a look at what you spend annually on entertainment. This can include movies, concerts and even vacations and is an often overlooked area that is perfect for shifting locally. Maybe once a month you make a point to do something fun in your community. Whether it's visiting a local museum, seeing a play at the town theater or dancing the night away at a local club. Entertainment might not always be the biggest spending area of your budget but having a little fun while helping out community businesses at the same time is highly satisfying.

> **SHOP LOCAL TIP**
>
> **Make the Shop Local Loop**
>
> Get out and drive or walk a one-mile radius around your neighborhood. Write down all the local shops you see and what services or products they offer to your community. Making the Shop Local Loop helps you scout your local indie stores, restaurants, boutiques and services you might have missed in your own neighborhood. This will help you find what you need closer to home.

WHERE TO FIND LOCAL INDIE BUSINESSES

In addition to actually getting out and visiting the local places in your town, you'll need to find out who are the local independents in your area. Below is a list of resources that can help you get started from the comfort of your own home.

Note: These are terrific resources to use to find your local businesses, but they may not be exclusive to local independents. So your search results may include regional and national chains or other big-box stores in your area. You still might want to visit the business website to check them out to determine whether they're an independent.

Community Publications. Beyond your city newspaper, there are probably a number of community and neighborhood publications available in print or online. Some of these are free and may even be delivered to your mailbox regularly. Before you toss these out as junk mail, take a moment to check them out. They will most likely contain advertisements or coupons for many local indie merchants or services. They may also highlight local activities in your area—and provide local places of interest.

Social Networks, Review Sites and Apps. Review sites like Yelp or CitySearch are helpful resources for finding businesses in your neighborhood. You may also want to visit Foursquare, GoWalla, Google Places, Yellow Pages, Living Social, as well as Facebook and Twitter to get to know more about those businesses. There are also many useful SmartPhone Apps based on these sites as well as others that feature businesses in your neighborhood (or wherever you happen to be with your SmartPhone) including Urban Spoon and Open Table for restaurants, Happy Hours for local places to eat, drink and be merry as well as inBloom which finds organic, environmental and sustainable businesses near your current location.

Chamber of Commerce. You can also visit your city's Chamber of Commerce website to find local indie businesses as well as professional service providers in your area. Most chambers are good about listing all of their participating members' contact information and details about their business at the chamber's website or they may publish a directory of members that you can request from the chamber directly.

Search for Shop Local initiatives in your area. More and more communities are creating their own Shop Local movements. There may even be one in your area. The Institute for Local Self-Reliance highlights "Buy Local" and "Local First" programs and initiatives throughout the United States. A map of all the local movements across the country is provided at their website. The American Independent Business Alliance is another helpful website for locating affiliates that list local indie businesses in their towns.

It just takes a little bit of research to find the local indie businesses in your area. Then all you need to do is choose where you want to shop in order to start supporting your local businesses and to reach your Shop Local goals.

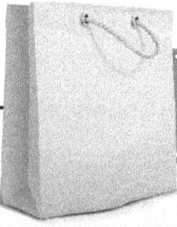

Think Local First

The biggest assumption I hear about shopping local is that small local retailers just can't compare to the big chains when it comes to selection. Because of the overall larger inventory, we go to the larger stores expecting to find exactly what we're looking for. But this is not always the case.

A friend of mine was recently searching for a gift for his wife; a blue ski jacket that she wanted for the holidays. Assuming the local retailers in his small 28 square-mile town wouldn't have the jacket, he took a 35-minute trip to another city headed to a big-box sporting goods store. Hoping to find a selection of sizes and colors to choose from, the store did not have the size he needed.

He then spent hours browsing at online stores searching for the perfect jacket, but had no luck. Finally, he stopped by his local retail store, surprised to find the jacket in the exact size and color his wife wanted. He also discovered there were actually two other retailers located less than 15 minutes away from his home that carried the same jacket he was looking for.

The Shop Local lesson here is to not dismiss the local indie stores in your neighborhood. Check with your local stores. They might have equal or even better selection than the big-box stores.

CHAPTER SIX
Sources of Inspiration

I am of the opinion that my life belongs to the community, and as long as I live it is my privilege to do for it whatever I can.

— GEORGE BERNARD SHAW

Whenever I set out to do something big, I often ask myself the rhetorical question: *So how do you eat an elephant?* The answer: *One bite at a time.* Not that I'd ever actually consider eating an elephant—heaven forbid—but the answer helps put my detail obsessed introverted mind back into first gear and reminds me that I can only meet my goals by taking one step at a time. By taking this approach, you'll achieve more than if you try to reach all of your goals by doing too much at once.

For my own Shop Local Shift, I first started thinking about what I loved about my town—friendly people, low crime, healthy lifestyle, community events, many choices for places to eat and explore. I don't want to lose any of these community attributes. Over the fifteen years that I've lived here, the city has had its financial ups and downs and local businesses have come and gone. I thought about how I could help sustain the character of my community.

I decided that I'd pick one thing I could do or buy locally each month. The first month, it was going out for Sunday dinner at the local Italian restaurant rather than ordering in from the national pizza chain. The next month, it was signing up for a membership with a Community Supported Agriculture group in my state to get fresh veggies. Then I stepped up my game and decided that I'd try to make at least one Shop Local purchase for anything I had to buy on any given day. This didn't mean that I started spending more money. It meant that whenever I did buy something using the money that was already in my budget, I'd commit to spending it locally.

The key is to start by choosing small actionable and achievable goals. Maybe you've decided that you're going to support the local businesses in your community by going to an indie café or restaurant every month. This is good. Maybe you add another goal next month. Try to make it a routine for yourself to consider how you can bring your Shop Local mission into frequent celebrations or events such as birthdays, anniversaries, holidays, girls' night out or guys' night out. Now, let's focus on how you can easily take action.

SET DAILY INTENTIONS

You've set your goals and you can't wait to get started with your Shop Local Shift. Now it's up to you to take action and stay committed because you know the payoff is going to have sweet rewards for you personally and for those in your community. So how do you stay focused?

One way to help you stay mindful of your Shop Local goals is by creating daily intentions. Daily intentions are mini goals which will help you keep your priorities in focus and plan your day.

Here's how it works: Before heading off to work or while you're out for your morning walk with the dog, take a few minutes to set your daily intentions to help you meet your Shop Local goals for the day. Ask yourself *What purchase decisions will I need to make today?* Can I direct my buying decisions or shopping activities toward a local business?

Maybe your day looks like this:

You're meeting a friend for coffee that morning and you're taking a client to lunch. Perhaps you need to buy a new outfit for a fancy soirée or you're planning a date night without the kids.

These are all opportunities for you to Shop Local.

For each of the buying decisions that you have to make that day, try to point your intentions toward taking action on your goals. Using our example, let's say you decide that rather than meeting your friend at the nearest Starbucks for coffee, you recommend a smaller café in town which you've never tried or you haven't been to in a while. Or you've planned a date night and you decide rather than running in to the supermarket on the way home from work to pick up a bouquet of flowers, you take a few minutes to find a local flower shop which you'll actually be passing by during your drive home. Stopping by a local indie flower shop—and not having to wait in line at the supermarket behind the other homeward-bound grocery shoppers—may be a better use of your time and might even put you in a better mood for date night.

Setting your daily intentions and writing them down helps you stay persistently mindful of your Shop Local mission as you're going about your day. To help me stay focused, I have *Shop Local* written on my whiteboard at work. Each day, I list the intentions that I set for myself that morning on my white board. Then I pick one or maybe two things that mean the most to me or may be easiest for me to do that day or during the week. Doing this helps remind me of my values and goals to support my community and my commitment to make at least one purchase from a local indie business when I have to buy something on any given day.

Whatever your daily intentions are, be sure that you put them somewhere prominent like a whiteboard or even on post it notes on your car dashboard, so that you'll see them every day as inspirational Shop Local reminders.

GET INSPIRED

I haven't always been a big fan of the vision board thing, but I have to admit that I've fallen in love with the large cork board that hangs on the wall in my office. It's filled with photos, news articles, mailers and note cards—all of these things inspire me and are reminders take action on something. So I've also created a Shop Local board at home where I post fliers or coupons that come in the mail for local businesses which may be of interest to me or that I might need later. Now, whenever I come across an article, review or advertisement featuring a local business in my area, I pin it on my Shop Local board.

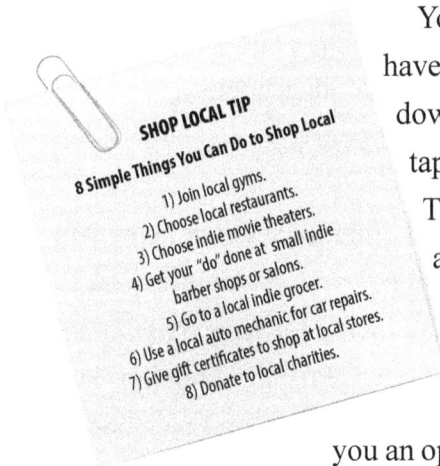

SHOP LOCAL TIP

8 Simple Things You Can Do to Shop Local

1) Join local gyms.
2) Choose local restaurants.
3) Choose indie movie theaters.
4) Get your "do" done at small indie barber shops or salons.
5) Go to a local indie grocer.
6) Use a local auto mechanic for car repairs.
7) Give gift certificates to shop at local stores.
8) Donate to local charities.

Your own Shop Local Board doesn't have to be clippings or ads. You may write down some of your daily intentions and tape them to your refrigerator door. These are ways to inspire you to achieve your goals. Starting a Shop Local board online at Pinterest. com is another fun way to visually inspire you to Shop Local, giving you an opportunity to share your commitment to supporting local businesses with many other people. Now you're influencing others to Shop Local too!

FIND SUPPORTERS

It helps to be around others who are on the same page or are also passionate about shopping local. Think about the people in your life at home, at work or friends who are supportive or can help you meet your goals. Maybe you can inspire each other to Shop Local together.

At home, get together with a group of neighbors or friends who may want to join you on walks to your local stores or to events in your town. Set some goals together with this group to create new local shopping traditions or competitions to see who can make the biggest Shop Local Shift. Then celebrate at the end of the year with a potluck.

At work, find some co-workers who might be interested in finding new low-cost local indie restaurants near work so you can go there together for lunch and avoid the fast-food chains. Start your own Shop Local contest or start an informal group to share the local places that you've discovered each month. Find people who will come along with you on your Shop Local journeys.

MONITOR PROGRESS

Since I've committed to shopping local as often as I can, focusing on my Shop Local goals each month has made it more enjoyable for me to manage my money, reconcile my budget and take a close look at my own finances. I know what my budget is each month and I've made wiser choices about where to spend my money based on the Shop Local goals I've set.

Set an appointment with yourself each month to monitor your progress and reflect on what you've been able to accomplish. Use this time to check in and see how you're doing on your goals. Maybe you couldn't eat at your favorite local sushi bar that month, but you were able to buy a new cookbook you found at the local indie bookstore rather than buying it online. If you've gone off track, then this is the time to redirect yourself. Be sure to reward yourself for the goals you've achieved.

STEP-BY-STEP

Let's recap some of the steps you can take to keep you on the path of living out your Shop Local mission and reaching your Shop Local goals.

1. Figure out how much of your spending budget you're willing and able to shift locally (using the Shop Local Shift Calculator).
2. Decide where you can make the shift most easily and what will have the biggest total impact for you.
3. Commit to the Shop Local goals you've set.
4. Create a strategy for choosing which items you can buy locally.
5. Find local indie businesses that you'll support.
6. Identify any goals for which you absolutely will not bend in order to make an impact to Shop Local (e.g., I will only donate to my community charities).
7. Find acceptable alternatives when you cannot Shop Local and how you'll strive to support your goals in some other way.
8. Consider what type of spending shift will give you the greatest reward based on your values and beliefs (e.g., financial, personal, time or experiences).
9. Assess your Shop Local Shift monthly or even annually to see if you're on target with your goals or need to adjust.

10. Reach full-time Shop Local awareness in your daily actions.

By following the simple steps in this list, you can easily make your Shop Local Shift happen.

Throughout this section, you've focused on exploring your values and priorities. You've set your Shop Local goals with the intent to create new local spending habits. You should be clear about how you're going to shift your spending to support more of your local businesses. Now it's time for you to put your daily intentions into action. Get the support of your Shop Local buddies. Keep your goals visible and be sure to check your progress regularly. You're on your way to becoming a Shop Local maven.

Ask for Help

When you shop at a local store, don't be afraid to speak to those who work there. Impersonal big-box and chain stores tend to force us to stay in our guarded shells because we just want to go in, find what we need and get out.

We may think we just don't need help. We might not be able to find someone to help us in a big warehouse store or we're met by overbearing salespeople so we avoid them entirely.

Most local indie businesses do an excellent job of helping you solve a problem or find what you're looking for. Since they feature select items, they have a greater incentive to provide you with the information you need about the product or service to decide if you want to purchase.

In big-box stores, there are usually so many products, that the employees might not be able to speak to their quality or how they all work, so your shopping experience is limited to *what you see is what you get*.

Being a shy person, I've been "just looking" for years to avoid store clerks when I shopped. When I started paying more attention to my own shopping habits, I realized that I also needed to change my approach in the stores I go into and ask for help. I've found that I enjoy my shopping experience more and I also make people feel good about doing their job when I ask them for help.

Part 3

Love to Shop Local!

Full-Time Feel-Good Consciousness

Seeing things change in the community where I live and in the places that I love to visit reminds me not to take anything for granted. I appreciate what we have here now and what's been here before me. This makes me want to work harder to protect the things that I love about my community so that others can also appreciate them as well. This is why I decided to write this book. Finding ways to make a difference by helping spread the word and getting others to Shop Local makes me feel good. It's just one way of giving back to my community.

Knowing that the small daily differences that we can make will add up to big differences in the future is what inspires me to do more. So the last section of this book goes into why it feels good to Shop Local and what you can do to take your Shop Local mission further by helping in a bigger way.

CHAPTER SEVEN
Sharing the Benefits

I am often asked what can people do to become a good global citizen. I reply that it begins in your community.

—KOFI ANNAN

Now that you know how to Shop Local, let's explore why we love to Shop Local. In this section, we look at the ways in which shopping local positively affects you, your neighborhood and beyond. Some of these may seem obvious, but it helps to be reminded of the incredible positive impact you can make when you choose to spend your money at a local indie business. And if each person reading this book makes just one shift to Shop Local, then the impact is even greater!

SHOP LOCAL—WHY IT FEELS GOOD

We Shop Local because we want to support our local indie businesses and quite frankly it feels good. In fact, studies have found that people in communities with vibrant small businesses are healthier too.

In February 2012, a national study by sociologists at LSU and Baylor University reviewed over three-thousand counties and parishes in the United States and found that the counties with the most thriving small businesses also had healthier residents.

This finding is based on a few factors, including greater local indie business support for health-related programs and activities in their communities, local business owner loyalty to their employees, and having an overall entrepreneurial culture which fosters a can-do approach to solving problems in the community.

As you continue to live out your mission to Shop Local by supporting more local indie businesses, you have a greater opportunity to impact your community and inspire others to do the same. This ability to make a difference has a tremendous reward and reminds us that we're all connected and rely upon each other to sustain our communities.

NEIGHBORHOOD & COMMUNITY BENEFITS

Perhaps the greatest reason to Shop Local is how it benefits neighborhoods and the local community. Although we've become much more involved online in our daily lives, a great deal of our time is still spent living offline in our neighborhoods. And when the community thrives, so does its residents.

Shopping Local…

Protects local services. Small businesses open to support the demands of a community and to serve the needs of the local citizens who live and work in the neighborhood. Consistently supporting more local indie businesses helps stabilize the local economy, keeping our shopping centers, town malls and retail businesses on main street as vibrant and bustling areas. Since local indie businesses typically cluster around business areas and near chain stores too, they're vulnerable to closures of other surrounding stores. As other businesses shut down, the smaller businesses also begin to disappear. The more customers who frequent local indie businesses, the more likely the businesses can continue to persevere during the tough times thanks to a steady customer base.

Creates an identity. Local indie businesses give a community its identity by providing goods and services that are unique or even exclusive to the area. Why is this important? Have you ever been in a shopping mall and noticed that you were surrounded by nothing but chain stores? All of these chain stores look about the same and sell the same type of merchandise. You wouldn't be able to tell if you were shopping in Toledo or New York. A community with a number of diverse local indie merchants has more character. These one-of-a-kind businesses stand out from chain stores and are more interesting, giving the neighborhood a sense

of place which attracts residents and tourists to spend more money in the community.

Strengthens community. Owners of local indie businesses are typically residents in the same area in which they work. This means that they're likely to be active in the community and support local charities, schools, sports teams and other nonprofits. Therefore, they're invested in the health of the neighborhoods where their businesses are located because their success depends upon the local customers. These factors combined instill a strong sense of local pride and builds stronger bonds within the community.

Sustains jobs. Locally owned and operated small businesses boost local employment and job opportunities. As Michael Shuman points out in his book, *The Small-Mart Revolution*, chain stores alone cannot sustain local employment. The vitality of any neighborhood is dependent upon the number of jobs and revenue created by local businesses which goes back to supporting the community and local economy.

Stimulates growth & attracts others to the community. When local indie businesses thrive, they bring more money into the community. When it's proven that an area is beneficial to small businesses, then others will want to do business there too. This attracts entrepreneurs to the area and leads to an influx of creative people to the community, bringing in more jobs and more money. As more residents are attracted to an area, more local services, businesses and employment opportunities are needed, stimulating greater growth.

Is better for the environment. When community residents frequent local shops versus traveling to outlying areas, it cuts down on traffic congestion and the gas required when going to non-local stores. This is friendlier to the environment and may actually end up saving residents some gas money spent to travel outside of their neighborhoods. Plus, in many cases local indie businesses source goods from local or regional suppliers rather than having to rely on long distance, cross country or overseas transportation to deliver goods to their store. This results in less harmful greenhouse gas emissions being released into the environment.

Adds value to the community. People are attracted to happy and healthy communities. When a community is thriving, its residents are less likely to relocate to another area. An active local economy keeps long-time local residents in the community and attracts new residents to the area. This has a positive impact on the local real estate market and can help increase property value.

STATE & REGIONAL BENEFITS

The benefits of shopping local extend beyond the core of your local community and go toward supporting critical services in the state and region in which you live. Revenue from taxes paid by local businesses helps to balance out the taxes paid by individuals in order to maintain tax-funded programs and state services.

Shopping Local...

Lessens burden for taxpayers. Local wage earners earning part-time salaries or less than minimum wage require more assistance from the state which puts a bigger burden on taxpayers. A UC Berkeley study found that California taxpayers spent $86 million a year in 2004 for healthcare and other public assistance, such as food stamps and subsidized housing, for the 44,000 Walmart employees in the state. Supporting local indie businesses that pay their employees sufficient wages and provide benefits would help reduce some of the taxpayer burden.

Increases revenue for state services. Most people gripe about paying sales tax. But a state sales tax goes toward funding numerous public services and improvements which our cities need to survive such as education, healthcare, transportation, correctional programs and public assistance. Without enough funds to support major public service programs, then sales taxes might be increased or funds may be raised through some other means of taxation. Or even worse, the services will cease entirely. Many big-box and retail chains may also get tax breaks as incentives to open up a store in a community which means fewer dollars are going to support the services in the areas where they do business. Online retailers can skirt state sales tax if the seller is based outside of your own state. While this battle is still being waged between individual states and Internet retailers, the net current effect is that there may be no money going to your state or region at all when you buy from an out-of-state online retailer. When you shop at a local indie business, more of your money goes toward your state's tax-funded programs and benefits the community.

PERSONAL BENEFITS

It's incredibly gratifying to support local indie businesses in your community. One of the most enlightening aspects of shopping local is that it makes you explore your neighborhood in a purposeful way. Not only will you meet your neighbors, you'll learn to love the area in which you live by getting to know the people behind the local businesses and discover how they contribute to the spirit of your community.

When you Shop Local, you...

Enhance your shopping experience. When you visit a local shop, you can see, touch, smell or even taste the product you intend to buy. You can interact with the people offering services and with the products sold at the business. If you're shopping online, you don't get the same experience. For me, I've been repeatedly disappointed with the online shopping experience. Too many times I'd try to guess if what I was buying was the right size based on their photos online, only to end up having to return them and then try to find the right product all over again. Now I'd much rather save time in the long run by seeing, trying or testing out an item in person at my local store.

Discover new local businesses. Many local shops are concentrated in high-traffic areas. So if you head to your local neighborhood pharmacy, for example, you may discover a quaint little Thai restaurant on the way. You may find a new hair salon or clothing boutique which just opened up. Sometimes the best new discoveries happen when you're out shopping local. By visiting your local indie merchants, you'll find new places that might suit your needs better than a chain or online store.

Can maximize your time. When you're out shopping in your local community, not only are you closer to home, but you can also find other ways to maximize your time while you're out. A visit to the local deli for lunch may inspire you to finally sign up for yoga classes at the studio next door to work off that potato salad later. Going into town to buy a gift for mom's birthday might remind you to get a quick hair cut while you're out at the local barber shop you passed by on the way.

Connect with people in your neighborhood. Most local indie businesses are owned and operated by people who live right in your neighborhood. When you frequent these local merchants, you'll expand your connections in the community. Feeling connected is a human need. Our reliance on each other grows as societies become more complex, interconnected and specialized. Connection is a prerequisite for survival, physically and emotionally. By going to shop at your local businesses, you can create a closer relationship with neighbors whom you otherwise might have never known.

Enjoy personalized service. Since local retail businesses often have fewer employees as compared to larger stores, they tend to look for those workers who are more skilled and personable. Chances are you're more likely to encounter an employee (or the owner herself) who actually knows a great deal about the business and the products or services at a local indie business. In my town, there's a local store that sells custom jewelry designed by local artists. The owner is able to have the artists change out a stone or adjust a piece to better suit her customers' tastes. This high level of personalization is what has kept her in business for over 15 years.

Encourage more choice in your community. When a local business community thrives, this encourages more new businesses to open up creating a greater number of choices for people to shop at in your neighborhood. By spending your money at local businesses, you're sending a message that your community supports local commerce. This helps to attract other new and exciting businesses to open up in your town. The more small businesses that come to town, the more choices you'll have when you shop locally.

When you support your local businesses, knowing that your dollars are getting directly into the hands of the people whom you actually see working there—and maybe even people you actually know in your neighborhood—is an incredibly gratifying reason to Shop Local. The people who own or work for those businesses will also be putting money their back into the community—business owners pay their employees who in turn spend money locally, leases for business locations get paid to local landlords and so on. These are all reasons why we love to Shop Local. And I'm sure you'll discover other reasons for yourself.

Now let's look at some other ways you can support your local businesses and share the Shop Local LOVE.

Find a Shop Local Buddy

You'll have more success reaching your Shop Local goals if you're not doing it alone. Find a friend or group of friends to take up the Shop Local cause together.

With a Shop Local buddy, you can keep each other accountable for your new goals and creating new local habits to get out and explore your neighborhood together. Seek out new shops and activities together or suggest to go to new local places you've heard about.

To go even further, create a little friendly competition amongst your friends to see who actually supported the most local indie businesses each month. You can find Shop Local buddies in your area at ShopLocal.us.

CHAPTER EIGHT
Do Good Feel Good

Community is a sign that love is possible in a materialistic world where people so often either ignore or fight each other. It is a sign that we don't need a lot of money to be happy—in fact, the opposite.

—JEAN VANIER

Supporting local businesses doesn't always require spending money. You can help your local businesses by visiting them frequently even if you don't always buy something and by spreading the word to others about them. Word-of-mouth marketing is highly valuable for any business, but especially for your local indie businesses—some local indie business owners have told me that they don't do any advertising at all and get their business entirely by word of mouth. The more people who are talking about their products or services, the more likely they will attract customers. By simply taking the time to discover your local indie merchants, you're increasing your awareness of these businesses and are more likely to talk about these places with other people—getting them excited about shopping local in the process.

SPREAD THE WORD

If there's a local business that you absolutely love, then show your support. It's so easy to voice your opinion online and share this in your social circles. "Like" your local indie businesses' fan pages on Facebook or tweet about them. Give the local indie business a review on Yelp or any of the review sites you like. And don't be afraid to provide honest and thoughtful, constructive comments. This helps local indie businesses know how they can improve their service and learn what their customers like about them. Savvy businesses will recognize and even reward their most supportive and vocal fans or loyal followers. Post your Shop Local discoveries and goals on your Facebook page or tweet it. Get your BFFs and best buds involved by raising awareness about local businesses and your commitment to Shop Local. Your voice can help the Shop Local movement as much as your dollars.

Get your blog on

If you love to Shop Local and want to get others to support their communities or join a cause in your town, tell the world about it. Start up a blog and make this your place for sharing stories, inspiration, photos and resources. Let your Shop Local voice be heard.

DO MORE WINDOW SHOPPING

Yes, window shopping counts too. Perhaps your budget is a bit tight one month and you can't purchase the dress you've been longing for or you've held off on buying a new suit until your next paycheck. You can still enjoy a little local window shopping. Go out on a nice day and check out the local shops. Window shopping actually helps because it keeps you connected with what's going on in the neighborhood. Chat with the people who work at the store. Start building a relationship as a potential customer and a neighbor. You might find out that the store is having a special you just can't pass up or they may be offering free samples that day. The bottom line is that window shopping and paying a visit to local indie stores keeps your commitment to supporting local businesses top of mind and builds your connection with the community.

TAKE A STAYCATION IN YOUR TOWN

Planning your next week off? Well, you can support local businesses by taking a staycation and exploring your town like a tourist. Get out and walk to dinner or treat yourself to a cocktail at your local wine bar. Act like you're on your vacation at home. Shop at the boutiques you've never been to before. Take pictures and share them with others. Your staycation pictures are inspiring for others to explore their own towns or it may get them to come out to discover what's in your town.

> **SHOP LOCAL TIP**
> **Buy your books at local indie bookstores**
>
> Local indie bookstores are having a bit of a renaissance serving the people out there who still prefer to hold a book in their hand and turn real pages rather than read on a mobile device. Even if you love your Kindle or Nook, there's something comforting about browsing through the books at these stores and many indie bookstores feature opportunities to meet local authors. Find links to local indie bookstore locators listed at the end of this book.

The more you're reminded of what you enjoy about the local indie businesses in your neighborhood, the more you'll stick to your Shop Local goals.

SHOP LOCAL WHEN YOU TRAVEL

You can also Shop Local when you travel. Some of my fondest memories have been made on road trips and during vacations when I've been able to go off the beaten path to discover amazing little stores or places to eat that aren't on the typical tourist itinerary. When you're on vacation, ask other tourists or locals about the places they recommend. Look out for interesting or unusual roadside stops while you're out on the highway in other cities and towns and pay them a visit. These smaller out of the way places often depend entirely on local tourists and other travelers to keep their businesses alive.

BRING SHOP LOCAL GOODNESS TO WORK

Inspire others while you work. Lead an event to encourage your coworkers to Shop Local. See if you can hold a contest at work and reward the employee who makes the biggest Shop Local Shift. Rewards don't have to be expensive. In fact, it could be a homemade dessert or trophy, a handmade award or a gift card for a local indie coffee house. Become the Shop Local leader at your office or within your organization. This will help your company stand out in the local business community and you'll be able to support your cause while having some fun at work.

GIVE LOCAL

Find your local town charities or organizations that are aligned with your favorite causes and support them. Give donations to smaller localized charities that you know are doing good work in your community. You can donate money that you already budget each year for charities or you can donate items you no longer need to your local second-hand store or thrift store. One of the things I love to do is declutter and get rid of what I no longer need. I can gather up several bags of clothing or household items to donate to my local thrift store, community center or church. Knowing that these items are going directly to someone else in my neighborhood who's able to use them makes me feel incredible.

KEEP IT GREEN

Shopping local can also be a great way to be green. Not only can you reduce your carbon footprint by driving shorter distances to local stores, you can even walk or bike to them to buy products that are locally produced and grown. Another way to be more eco-friendly is to shop at local indie second-hand or antique stores. Buying gently used or recycled items from local indie stores is green because you're actually reusing something. I've found some of the best items for my home at these shops. I enjoy my archeological-like digs in search of the perfect table or the retro sixties crock pot my mom used to make her pot roast in. You can also save some money when shopping at local indie thrift stores. I'll never forget the used green couch I bought for my first apartment at the local thrift store for only $60.

GET INVOLVED WITH THE COMMUNITY

See if you can volunteer or offer to lead a Shop Local campaign in your community. Find local civic groups that support commerce and local business events in town and get involved. Local nonprofit boards and other business groups are also looking for people to help them as leaders, decision makers and organizational support. Reach out to these groups to express your enthusiasm. Share your experience and what skills you bring to the table so they know what you can offer.

LEAD BY EXAMPLE

Your actions and decisions to make a Shop Local Shift and support local indie businesses can influence other people to do the same. Spread the message of shopping local to others by simply doing it.

Here are a few suggestions to inspire your friends, family or kids to Shop Local:

- Skip McDonald's and take your family to a locally owned burger place.
- Meet friends at a community coffee shop instead of Starbucks.
- Visit a local museum instead of a major theme park.
- Spend an afternoon walking around local shopping areas or markets in town versus visiting the mall.
- Try out a new and exciting indie restaurant in your community at least once a month.
- Invite local people including local indie professionals or business owners you know to join you socially so they can mix with your friends.

When you make shopping local part of your everyday life, then other people will also take notice. They might make their own shift and begin to Shop Local. And hopefully, they'll begin to feel the benefits of shopping local as you have.

BE PERSISTENTLY MINDFUL

Shopping local is something I continue to work on each day. It's easy to fall back into old habits and shop at the big-box stores because you may not have to think as much. But I've found that when I set my daily intentions and continue to blend more local shopping into my life, the easier it becomes.

Now before I buy anything, I always ask myself *Where can I find this locally?*

If I don't know, then I look it up online or visit my Shop Local board to see if I might already have something posted there that can help me find what I'm looking for.

Then I ask *Is this something unique that I can't find easily? Or is it a common item and my priority is to find the cheapest price or best quality? Can I find something better, different or just as great at my local stores?*

Some of these questions may go through your mind already when you shop, but by paying closer attention to them from a Shop Local perspective, you can get into the practice of being more locally mindful in your purchase decisions. With persistence and practice, all of this will become second nature to you.

There are many directions you can take to make a difference based on all the ideas shared in this section. Perhaps you may find it a bit overwhelming. But the first step begins by looking at what matters most to you. Which of these ideas get you excited about taking action? Think about how you can incorporate this into your daily life. You can become the Shop Local activist in your town and inspire others to Shop Local. Or just make a Shop Local spending shift that makes you feel good.

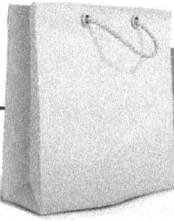

Have Some Local Fun

Looking for ways to have fun in your own town? Try doing at least one or two fun things per month as part of your Shop Local goals. Here are some ideas for you to try:

1. Browse at the local bookstore.
2. Visit the local art gallery.
3. Take a class from the local art studio or music store.
4. Listen to a live local band.
5. Sign up for a dance class.
6. Inspire your inner muse by perusing the local craft or bead shop.
7. See a matinée at an indie theater in your town.
8. Buy your flowers at a local nursery.
9. Start a Shop Local walking group in your community.
10. Take a second-language class at the local community center.

CHAPTER NINE
Shop Local Tips You Can Use Now

You are only one thought away from changing your life.

—RITA SCHIANO

Throughout this book, I've offered suggestions and ideas you can use to make your Shop Local Shift. Here are a few tips that will not only enhance your experience when connecting with your local indie businesses but can help you meet your goals. There are twelve of them, so you can you can pick one to do each month or you can use this as a checklist for monitoring your progress on your Shop Local Shift.

SHOP LOCAL TIP #1: START WITH ONE ITEM

An easy way to begin shopping local is to choose just one item you purchase regularly and then buy it locally. Make a list of what you buy every month from a big-box store. It can be anything like food, clothing, household supplies or even a service like housekeeping or gardening. Pick one item you can easily find at a local indie business and make the switch. Starting with one item is so easy that you'll want to do more.

SHOP LOCAL TIP #2: EAT AT LOCAL PLACES

One of the easiest ways to keep your money in the community is by eating at your locally owned neighborhood restaurants. For each meal you enjoy locally, you're also helping that business stay open to serve the community and provide jobs for people in your neighborhood.

SHOP LOCAL TIP #3: EAT LOCAL STUFF

Try to buy locally grown fruits, veggies and other homemade specialty foods direct from your local farmers market or direct from local growers through Community Supported Agriculture groups. When you do shop at the supermarket, try to buy items that are local or at least regional. Read the labels to see how local your produce or food items are before you buy. Another great way to support local indie businesses when grocery shopping is by buying from the independent grocery stores in your neighborhood. There are over 5,000 indie grocery stores in the United States You can find them at the Independent Grocers Alliance (IGA) website at www. iga.com/consumer or at the National Grocers Association (NGA) website, you can look for the local indie grocers in your state at www.nationalgrocers.org/member-center/member-directory.

SHOP LOCAL TIP #4: DRINK LOCAL

The next time you're buying beverages at your local store, take a closer look at the label. Where is the beverage produced? Try to seek out beverages that are produced or bottled closer to home. Take a trip to wine country to buy regional wines. Look for locally brewed beers or brew houses in your town. You can also drink local at the indie pubs or coffee houses in your area to support your neighborhood baristas and bartenders.

SHOP LOCAL TIP #5: MAKE THE SHOP LOCAL LOOP

Sure, you can discover local shops and services online. But it's better when you discover them by getting out and exploring your community. There are interesting places that we pass by all the time in our towns but never think twice about visiting. Make a point to discover local indie businesses by driving (or walking) a one-mile loop around your neighborhood to get to know what's in your town.

SHOP LOCAL TIP #6: FIND A SHOP LOCAL BUDDY

Shopping is always easier and more fun to do with a friend or two. Find some friends with whom you can make the Shop Local Shift together. Motivate each other to find local indie alternatives to chain stores in town. It will keep you on track with your shift and you'll start a Shop Local mini-movement in your own circle of friends.

SHOP LOCAL TIP #7: THINK LOCAL BEFORE YOU SHOP

Before you buy something, first ask yourself *Can I find what I need right in my own backyard?* When you shop, try to find where you can buy what you need closer to home. Don't always assume that the local stores in your town won't have what you need because they're smaller. Bigger isn't always better. Check with your local indie stores first before you head to the big chain store or start to shop online.

SHOP LOCAL TIP #8: USE LOCAL SERVICES

The next time you need a car repair or home repair done, choose a local service provider over a chain or large franchise service. Or maybe you need a dentist or an accountant. Look to local service providers in your neighborhood to help you. Your best referrals will come from nearby friends, coworkers and family. Or you can use online review sites like Yelp and Service Magic to find a provider in your area.

SHOP LOCAL TIP #9: FIND LOCAL ENTERTAINMENT

Dinner and a movie can get a little boring after a while—and expensive. Why not find some other way to be entertained in your local community? I'll bet there are many fun things to do in your neighborhood. The next time you want to have a little fun, go to a local theater production, sporting event or see what's on exhibit at your nearby museum. Maybe buy a sandwich from your local deli and picnic at the park, take a class at the town recreational center or catch a live local band. Local entertainment calendars can be found online or in your local paper and are often quite easy on the budget and many local events serve as fundraisers for community programs and charities.

SHOP LOCAL TIP #10: SWITCH BANKS

Keep your savings or your loans with local indie community banks or credit unions. When you bank local, more money stays local because the interest, the deposits or the loan payments you make help the bank to lend to local businesses or families in your community. These banks can offer the same capabilities as the big banks, but they concentrate on serving only one or two communities based on their smaller asset size. Since they're locally owned and focus on serving the businesses and families in their geographic area, they build up local wealth in your community. And there is usually greater stability in personnel at a community bank meaning that you'll likely be dealing with the same banker for years. A great resource to understand more about local indie banks is at the Independent Community Bank Association website. You can also use their locator tool to find community banks near you at www. icba.org/consumer/BankLocator.cfm?sn.ItemNumber=51757.

SHOP LOCAL TIP #11: ASK FOR HELP

When you shop at a local indie store don't hesitate to ask for help. It saves you time, you get to know more about a product or service before you buy it and you connect with the local people working there. Make a point to be a visible and engaged patron. While a good sales person will usually initiate a dialog with you, don't hesitate to do it first. Chatting with the people working there will make for a far more enjoyable experience and chances are you're engaging with somebody who also lives local. You'll be building relationships while you get the assistance you need when you shop.

SHOP LOCAL TIP #12: GIVE LOCAL GIFTS

Why give someone an item they can easily purchase on their own at the nearby big-box store? Maybe you saved them the time it would take them to buy it on their own, but your gift isn't unique or special. The next time you have to buy a gift for someone, take a different approach and give them a gift that's local. You'll surely find a unique gift at a smaller indie store and some stores may even feature items made by local artisans in the area. Plus, it showcases the essence of where you live.

As you check in each month on your progress with your Shop Local goals, note which of these tips you've actually applied that month. If you've followed the steps outlined in this book, you'll probably find that you've taken action on at least one if not several of these ideas intuitively.

Shopping local will come to mean different things to different people. Some will make small changes in their lives, others might make big ones. Some may do nothing at all. I hope, at the very least, that I've planted a seed in your mind to think before you buy and that I've given you the tools to help you decide how and where you want to spend your money. I hope you're inspired to take an even closer look at the local indie businesses in your own backyard.

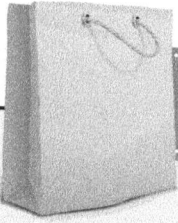

Those That Give Back

Part of the Shop Local Shift is about being more aware of what's happening in your neighborhood. Charity and sponsored events are happening all the time in towns everywhere. Look for those local indie businesses that often participate at local community events or donate to charitable causes— this is the multiplier effect in action.

You can do this by reading the local news, chatting with your neighbors and paying closer attention to fund raisers and dedications happening around town at your local schools, hospitals and hosted at local indie businesses.

It's always best to support a business that gives back to the community where it's based. Getting to know the businesses in your town that actively support local citizens and causes also helps you decide where to Shop Local and which local indie businesses are truly worthy of your business.

CONCLUSION

This guide is meant to help you find meaningful ways to shop and strengthen your local economy—all while gaining a greater sense of pride for your community. Apply the ideas that appeal most to you and commit to your goals—either by making a Shop Local Shift, trying the Shop Local Loop or coming up with new ideas of your own. Celebrate your successes and feel good about what you're doing to support local indie businesses in your town. Your choices have a profound impact on the world around you, so enjoy this experience by sharing it with others and leaving a legacy.

Shopping local has been an incredibly rewarding journey for me and writing this book has been a pleasure. I hope that I've inspired you to find ways to adopt shopping local as part of your everyday life. Stay connected and share your success stories from your own Shop Local journeys on our blog site at *HeidiShopsLocal.com*. Join the Shop Local movement at *ShopLocal.us* and help your favorite local indie businesses get recognized by the movement by letting us know about them.

Thank you for reading my book. Here's to shopping local and making a difference.

ABOUT THE AUTHOR

Heidi Butzine is a best-selling author, entrepreneur, wine aficionado and shop local maven who loves helping businesses succeed. Her most recent book, *Shop Local: A Practical Pain-Free Guide to Shopping with Purpose,* is the result of extensive, hands-on research and part of her personal mission to get more people to support local businesses everywhere and strengthen the communities where they work and live. Her dedication to the shop local movement has been inspired by her work as the creator of the *Wineopolis Citizen's Guide* wine travel book series, written to encourage local tourism and commerce. Heidi is the founder of ShopLocal.us and the Certified Locally Owned[TM] program. She is a native Californian and lives in Redondo Beach, California..

REFERENCES

Basker, Emek. Job Creation or Destruction? (2005, February). Labor-Market Effects of Wal-Mart Expansion. *Review of Economics & Statistics*. University of Missouri. Retrieved from http://www.ilsr.org/key-studies-walmart-and-bigbox-retail.

Boarnet, Dr. Marlon & Crane, Dr. Randall. (1999). The Impact of Big Box Grocers on Southern California: Jobs, Wages, and Municipal Finances. Prepared for the *Orange County Business Council*. The University of California at Irvine and the University of California at Los Angeles. Retrieved from http://www.ilsr.org/key-studies-walmart-and-bigbox-retail.

California Department of Food and Agriculture. *Certified Farmers Market Program*. See http://www.cdfa.ca.gov/is/i_&_c/cfm.html.

Cortese, Amy. (2011). *Locavesting: The Revolution in Local Investing and How to Profit from it*. Hoboken, NJ: John Wiley & Sons, Inc.

Davis, Julie, Merriman, David, et al. (2009, December). The Impact of an Urban Wal-Mart Store on Area Businesses: An Evaluation of One Chicago Neighborhood's Experience. Research report prepared and published by the *Center for Urban Research and Learning, Loyola University*. Retrieved from http://laborcenter.berkeley.edu/retail/walmart.pdf.

Dube, Arindrajit T. & Jacobs, Ken. (2004, August 2). Hidden Cost of Wal-Mart Jobs: Use of Safety Net Programs by Wal-Mart Workers in California. *UC Berkeley Labor Center and UC Berkeley Institute for Industrial Relations*. Retrieved from http://laborcenter.berkeley.edu/retail/walmart.pdf.

Dube, Arindrajit T., Lester, Willam & Eidlin, Barry. (2007, December). A Downward Push: The Impact Of Wal-Mart Stores On Retail Wages And Benefits. *UC Berkeley Center for Labor Research and Education.* Retrieved from http://laborcenter.berkeley.edu/retail/walmart_downward_push07.pdf.

Estimating the Economic Impact of Public Markets. (2007, February). Report Submitted To: *Project for Public Spaces.* Prepared by Econsult Corporation. Retrieved from http://www.pps.org/reference/measuring-the-impact-of-public-markets-and-farmers-markets-on-local-economies.

Farmers Market Integrity. (2010, October 30). *KCRW Talk Radio Online.* Good Food. Los Angeles. 11:08AM. Retrieved from http://www.kcrw.com/etc/programs/gf/gf101030haunted_la_restauran.

Hamilton, Neil D. (2002, June). An Agricultural Law Research Article Farmers' Markets Rules, Regulations and Opportunities. *National Center for Agricultural Law Research and Information.* University of Arkansas School of Law. Retrieved from http://www.nationalaglawcenter.org/assets/articles/hamilton_farmersmarkets.pdf.

How Big are Big-Box Stores? *Institute for Local Self Reliance.* See www.ilsr.org/how-big-are-bigbox-stores.

Jolly, Desmond and Eckert, Eileen. (2005). The Farmers Market Management Series: Volume 1. Starting a New Farmers Market. *UC Small Farm Center, Davis California.* Chapters 1 through 16. Retrieved from http://sfp.ucdavis.edu/farmers_market/management1/chp1.pdf.

Living Wage Policies and Big-box Retail: How a Higher Wage Standard Would Impact Wal-Mart Workers and Shoppers. (2011, April). *UC Berkeley Center for Labor Research and Education.* Retrieved from http://laborcenter.berkeley.edu/livingwage/

Mitchell, Stacy. (2000, April 18). The Impact of Chain Stores on Community. *Institute for Local Self Reliance*. Retrieved from www.ilsr. org/retail/article/impact-chain-stores-community.

Parsons, Russ (2006, May 24). The idea that shook the world. Farmers Markets/The Movement. *Los Angeles Times*. Retrieved from http://articles.latimes.com/2006/may/24/food/fo-farmer24.

Schwartz, Judith. (2009, June 11). Buying Local: How It Boosts the Economy. *Time Magazine*. Retrieved from http://www.time.com/time/business/article/0,8599,1903632,00.html.

Shuman, Michael. (2006, 2007). *The Small-Mart Revolution: How Local Businesses are Beating the Global Competition*. San Francisco, CA: Berrett-Koehler Publishers, Inc.

Slow Food Los Angeles Blog Site. (2012, November 2). *On the Integrity of our Farmers' Markets*. Retrieved from http://slowfoodla.com/2010/11/on-the-integrity-of-our-farmers-markets.

The Andersonville Study of Retail Economics. (2005, February). Prepared by *Civic Economics*. Chicago, Illinois. Retrieved from http://www.ilsr.org/key-studies-walmart-and-bigbox-retail.

The Multiplier Effect of Local Independent Business Ownership. *American Independent Business Alliance*. See www.amiba.net/resources/multiplier-effect.

Thinking Outside the Box: A Report on Independent Merchants and the New Orleans Economy. (2009, September). *The Urban Conservancy in partnership with Civic Economics*. Retrieved from http://www.livingeconomies.org/aboutus/research.

Time to Switch Drugstores? (2003, October). Published by the Consumers Union. Republished by *Consumer Reports* magazine.

United States Census Bureau (2008). *Statistics about Business Size (including Small Business)*, Table 2a. Employment Size of Employer and Nonemployer Firms. Retrieved from http://www.census.gov/econ/smallbus.html.

U.S. Counties With Thriving Small Businesses Have Healthier Residents. (2012, February 2). Baylor University. Republished by *ScienceDaily*. Retrieved from http://www.livingeconomies.org/aboutus/research.

USDA Agriculture Marketing Service. (2012, April 8). *Farmers Markets*. See http://www.ams.usda.gov/AMSv1.0/FARMERSMARKETS.

USDA Blog. (2011, September 21). *Listening Session Gives the Floor to Organic Community*. Posted by Miles McEvoy. Retrieved from http://blogs.usda.gov/2011/09/21/listening-session-gives-the-floor-to-organic-community.

USDA Blog. (2012, January 3). *Taking A Closer Look At the Benefits of Farmers Markets*. Posted by Jessica Milteer. See http://blogs.usda.gov/2012/01/03/taking-a-closer-look-at-the-benefits-of-farmers-markets/#more-37568.

Walmart local sourcing expert testifies before Senate Agriculture Committee. (2012, March 7). *Walmart Green Room*. Retrieved from www.walmartgreenroom.com/2012/03/walmart-local-sourcing-expert-testifies-before-senate-agriculture-committee.

ADDITIONAL RESOURCES

Locavesting: The Revolution in Local Investing and How to Profit From It by Amy Cortese

Local Dollars, Local Sense: How to Shift Your Money from Wall Street to Main Street and Achieve Real Prosperity--A Community Resilience Guide by Michael Shuman

The Small-Mart Revolution: How Local Businesses Are Beating the Global Competition by Michael Shuman

Inquiries Into the Nature of Slow Money: Investing as if Food, Farms, and Fertility Mattered by Woody Tasch

INDEPENDENT BUSINESS ALLIANCES AND ORGANIZATIONS

To find an alliance near you, visit AMIBA or BALLE.

The American Independent Business Alliance (AMIBA) is a non-profit organization helping communities launch and successfully operate an Independent Business Alliance (IBA), "buy independent, buy local" campaigns, forward pro-local policies, and other initiatives to support local entrepreneurs and vibrant local economies.

For more information, visit www.amiba.net.

The Business Alliance for Local Living Economies (BALLE) is North America's fastest growing network of socially responsible businesses, comprised of over 80 community networks in 30 U.S. states and Canadian provinces representing over 22,000 independent business members across the U.S. and Canada.

For more information, visit www.livingeconomies.org.

The Institute for Local Self-Reliance (ILSR) is a national research and policy organization founded in 1974 to advance community-centered, environmentally sound and equitable economic development.

For more information, visit www.ilsr.org.

National Trust for Historic Preservation is a national organization started in 1949 to provide support and encouragement for grass roots preservation efforts. Their National Main Street Center is focused on revitalizing communities and creating sustainable downtown and neighborhood commercial districts.

For more information, visit www.preservationnation.org/main-street.

WHERE TO FIND LOCAL INDIE BUSINESSES

ShopLocal.us

Go to www.shoplocal.us to find Certified Locally Owned^{TM} businesses in your area and get access to resources to make your Shop Local Shift including local indie business listings, farmers markets and Shop Local buddies. Take the free fun test to get your Shop Local IQ and brag to your friends. Show the world how much you're doing to support local indie businesses.

For more information, visit www.shoplocal.us.

Grocery Stores

The Independent Grocers Alliance (IGA) was founded in 1926, bringing together independent grocers across the United States to ensure that the trusted, family-owned local grocery store remained strong in the face of growing chain competition.

Find local indie grocers at www.iga.com/consumer.

The National Grocers Association (NGA) is the national trade association representing the retail and wholesale grocers that comprise the independent sector of the food distribution industry.

Find more local indie grocers at www.nationalgrocers.org/member-center/member-directory.

Bookstores

The American Booksellers Association is a national, not for profit trade association, and exists to protect and promote the interests of its members: independently owned bookstores, large and small, with storefront locations in towns and cities nationwide.

Find local indie bookstores at www.indiebound.org or visit www. bookweb.org/aba/members/search.do.

Banks/Financial Institutions

The Independent Community Bankers of America is dedicated exclusively to representing the interests of the community banking industry and its membership through effective advocacy, best-in-class education and high-quality products and services. The organization represents over 7,000 community banks.

Find local community banks at www.icba.org/consumer/ BankLocator.cfm?sn.ItemNumber=51757.

Professional Services

Angie's List is a word-of-mouth network for consumers based on a growing collection of homeowners' real-life experiences with local service companies. The service receives more than 40,000 reports each month about the companies they've hired.

For more information, visit www.angieslist.com.

Index

ABOUT SIMPLEX PUBLISHING

Simplex Publishing is an independent publisher dedicated to publishing books and other media that inspire us to improve ourselves and our communities through learning and self-discovery. Built by experienced self-publishing partners and authors, the Simplex name reflects our mission to take the complex process of writing and publishing and make it simple. Committed to making the finest publications possible, we help aspiring writers fulfill dreams to publish high-quality books without having to do it all alone.

CONNECT WITH US

Visit Our Website

Go to www.shoplocal.us to find Certified Locally Owned^{TM} businesses in your area and get access to resources to make your Shop Local Shift including local indie business listings, farmers markets and Shop Local buddies. Take the free fun test to get your Shop Local IQ and brag to your friends. Show the world how much you're doing to support local indie businesses.

Follow the Author's Blog

Stay connected with the author and Shop Local community at her blog www.heidishopslocal.com for more stories, tips and inspiration from her Shop Local discoveries.

Cobrand This Book for Your Business

Show your commitment to local indie businesses in your community by cobranding the *Shop Local* book with your company or organization's name. Share this book proudly with your members, customers and clients as a token of your support. Please contact us at sales@simplexpublishing.com.

Shop Local.
Shop Smart.
Look for the Badge.

Certified Locally Owned™ is an exclusive certification
for independently owned businesses.

★

Certification helps conscious consumers find and buy from local
independent companies and professionals based in their area.

Join the movement...

★ Business Owners:

Sign up for your certification online and let us help you boost your visibility
and gain local attention. It's like getting an award that helps your business
stand out from the rest by touting your independence.

★ Passionate Shoppers:

We honor our friends who help us spread the word in their communities.
Encourage your friends to certify their small business and earn an
American Express Gift Card for each business that signs up and qualifies.

Help your favorite local businesses stand out from the competition. Get on
board with the power of ShopLocal.us to increase support for local
business, build community and local pride. -- It's fun and it's easy.

Learn more at certifiedlocallyowned.com

www.ingramcontent.com/pod-product-compliance
Lightning Source LLC
LaVergne TN
LVHW011239080426
835509LV00005B/553